NO HERO

ALSO BY MARK OWEN
with Kevin Maurer

*No Easy Day: The Firsthand Account
of the Mission That Killed Osama bin Laden*

NO HERO

The Evolution of a Navy SEAL

Mark Owen

with Kevin Maurer

DUTTON

→ est. 1852 ←

DUTTON
⟶ est. 1852 ⟵

Published by the Penguin Group
Penguin Group (USA) LLC
375 Hudson Street
New York, New York 10014

USA | Canada | UK | Ireland | Australia | New Zealand | India | South Africa | China
penguin.com
A Penguin Random House Company

Photographs in the insert are from the author's collection.

LIBRARY OF CONGRESS CATALOGING-IN-PUBLICATION DATA
has been applied for.

ISBN 978-0-525-95452-1

Printed in the United States of America
1   3   5   7   9   10   8   6   4   2

Set in Adobe Garamond
Designed by Spring Hoteling

CONTENTS

CONTENTS

Publisher's Note

The author submitted this manuscript for review by the Defense Office of Prepublication & Security Review (DOPSR) at the United States Department of Defense. Some material not essential to the book was removed or rewritten during the review process. In some cases no agreement between the author and DOPSR could be reached, and in those instances the passages in question have been redacted. The names of all individuals in the book have been changed for their security.

The views expressed in this publication are those of the author and do not necessarily reflect the official policy or position of the Department of Defense or the U.S. government.

NO HERO

Forty Names

I was home in Virginia Beach on standby when the texts started coming in.

It was August 2011 and the city was packed with tourists. Every day I drove by people on vacation, heading to the ocean for a day on the beach. I stayed away from the Oceanfront—the area that runs parallel to the beaches—where the T-shirt shops and mini golf courses attract sunburned vacationers. The tourists were in a beach state of mind, but all I could think about was Afghanistan and my upcoming deployment.

The dog and pony show of dignitaries and political leaders was finally over. Now the prospect of going back overseas had me straining against a leash like a dog, ready to get back to work. But first I had to survive standby.

Standby was the worst.

It was one "spin" after another. We got a weekly brief on the latest intelligence from the world's hot spots, which actually made things worse. We all wanted to be working, conducting actual missions. But during standby, all we could do was plan for missions that would probably never happen. Overseas it was common to get a mission, put together a plan, and execute it a few hours later. But most of the operations we were involved in during standby were spur-of-the-moment contingency operations that would eventually disappear. We'd spin up, plan the operation, only to spin back down as Washington decided on another option, or the hot spot cooled off. Making it worse, we were living at home, but we had very little time actually being at home with family. We had to keep our families at arm's length because we never knew when we'd suddenly be gone. I'd stick them in the same compartment in my brain that I used during deployments. For me, I was gone during standby, even if my parents could call me on the phone.

I know it was the same for every teammate. We all just wanted to get into the action.

It was early evening and I'd just finished dinner. We weren't supposed to drink or party on standby. The last thing anybody wanted to do was show up drunk for a possible mission. I was looking at a lazy night in front of the TV when I received a series of text messages about a helicopter crash. The messages all read the same.

"There's a CH-47 down in Afghanistan. Ours?"

It was what we call "rumint," a mix of real news and rumor that oftentimes turned into bullshit. Unfortunately, this time it would turn out to be true.

I had to see only one text before my mind started turning. If it was true, it didn't matter if it was SEALs, Delta, or Special Forces. They were teammates in the same fight. I called a good friend of mine who was on the squadron that was overseas. He wasn't with his team because he was home taking care of his mother, who was sick. I thought he might know something.

No answer.

I kept scrolling through my phone, calling anyone who might have information. Then I got the confirmation.

"It was ours."

The news hit me like an electric charge. In my head, I could see all of my buddies in that squadron. My cell phone buzzed as the news spread. The same message kept coming up.

"It was ours."

My stomach hurt. I couldn't sit still. I paced in my kitchen, my head down, scrolling through texts, waiting for more information, but dreading each new piece. I knew my teammates had all volunteered countless times to be in that exact place, doing what they were doing. It could have easily been me in the helicopter. Hell, I'd been in a helicopter crash a few months earlier. It was harder being back at home waiting for word, a feeling most of our wives and girlfriends knew all too well.

After a while, I couldn't be alone. I grabbed a twelve-pack of beer from the fridge and walked down the street to a fellow SEAL's house. We were going to need a few beers tonight.

The sun was fading and the streets were deserted. As I walked the few blocks to my buddy's house, I looked around the neighborhood. The development was new, with few trees. Large brick houses sat on manicured lawns. On the weekends, I watched my neighbors stress over their lawns, mowing and manicuring the bushes to perfection. It made the streets look peaceful.

Most of my neighbors were oblivious to what I or any of the guys who came to my house did when they were at work. As I walked past the houses, I was sure my neighbors were thinking about summer vacation plans, bills, or what baseball game they were going to watch that night. It struck me how wide the chasm was between what was going on in Afghanistan and what was happening at home. I knew my neighbors cared and supported the troops, but they had no idea what it was like and how often my teammates risked their lives. The war was largely absent from daily life at home except for the families left behind to wait for their sailor or soldier to return.

They would never understand the amount of sacrifice being performed by our military on a daily basis. There was nothing I could do to change that, and tonight, it really didn't matter. The sacrifice was made. Now it was left to us to make sure it wasn't forgotten. The disconnect between those of us who put our lives on the line and the rest of the country was never as stark for me as it was on that quiet night.

When I got to my buddy's house, he opened the door with the same pained look on his face as I had. He just nodded and motioned me to come inside. I walked silently to his refrigerator and dropped off the beer. I grabbed two bottles and we quickly retreated to his back deck, leaving his family alone in the living room.

I popped off the top of my beer and took a long drink.

The beer didn't taste like anything. I was just seeking the effect. My buddy silently drank his and scrolled through the messages on his phone. We sat for a while. Neither of us spoke. The helicopter was full of our friends, and they were all lost. It was a paralyzing feeling because all we wanted was to act, but there was nothing we could do.

The sun had finally set, and it was completely dark on the deck. I could barely make out my buddy's face in the shadows. He didn't bother to turn on the back light. I think we were both glad for the darkness. It made the grieving a little easier.

For months politicians and the media had been celebrating the SEAL teams after the Osama bin Laden mission. I don't know how many times I'd heard the word "hero" thrown around. "Hero" is not a word we use easily, and it had gotten to the point where it had lost all meaning in our community. Everyone was a hero now.

The weight of the losses didn't really hit in earnest until names started to appear on my iPhone screen.

We tipped back beer after beer as we recounted stories about the guys on the helicopter. We both tried hard to remember the best stories, the funny stories, about each guy. There was no shortage. Humor gets us through the toughest and most stressful moments. We reached back in our memories for anything that would bring up a laugh. My buddy was inside grabbing a couple more beers when a new name popped up on my phone.

Ray.

It hit me like a gut punch. I set the phone down on the table and started to pace along the wooden boards of the deck. I met Ray for the first time in 1999 on the beach in San Diego. We were both about to start BUD/S, the SEAL training course. He'd been to college in Louisiana. He completed a year before giving in to his desire to be a SEAL. I had made it through college before I'd finally succumbed to the same life-long itch. I remember standing next to Ray in the sand, looking at the surf, and listening to the instructors yell at us. He looked determined, focused. All the noise and chaos didn't seem to affect him at all.

Ray came across as a bit quiet until you got to know him. Unlike me, he was a natural athlete. He had been a soccer player in high school, and he had that lean physique. Over time I would see Ray naturally excel at most of the physical challenges that the instructors could throw at him. What made him so solid was his consistency. He always finished whatever we were doing—a swim, a beach run, the obstacle course—at or near the front of the pack, no matter the conditions.

We both graduated BUD/S in December 1999. Ray was stationed at SEAL Team Three. I was assigned to SEAL Team Five. Since we were both based in San Diego, we saw each other as often as possible. However, with our busy schedules, we were usually on different sides of the globe.

Ray had a black cat's nine lives.

Some of his close calls had become legend. Ray got shot in the neck a few months before he screened for selection and training, or S&T. He was on a six-month deployment to Guam with SEAL Team Three. He and some of his friends had gone to a bar to celebrate Christmas. After a minor altercation with some locals, Ray and his fellow SEALs decided to call it a night. They climbed into a taxi and were headed back to the base when one of the guys from the bar, hanging out of the window of a nearby car, opened fire.

The bullets smashed into the taxi's windows. One of the bullets struck Ray in the neck, traveling clean through. Larry, another SEAL in the taxi, got hit in the ear. The bullet came out of his nose. The taxi driver rushed them both to the hospital. Ray stanched the blood with his shirt and walked into the emergency room for treatment.

A couple months later he showed up for S&T. He was in my class and we made it through together, but just like after BUD/S, we wound up assigned to different squadrons.

Now Ray was dead. I still didn't believe it.

My buddy came back with another round of beers, shaking me out of my funk. We sat for a few more minutes silently. We both had our phones out, scrolling through the messages. But I was still thinking about Ray.

"Hey," I said. "You ever see that footage of Ray in Afghanistan?"

My buddy gave a knowing chuckle.

"If it were me, I'd be dead," my buddy said.

Most mornings when we got into work and checked our email, there would be an After Action Review (AAR) waiting for us. An AAR is a report, sometimes including video footage from overhead drone coverage, generated by everyone involved in a mission. Everyone from the helicopter pilots to the intelligence analysts to the SEALs discussed all the things that went right and all the things that went wrong during the night's mission. These AARs were distributed within the community so that, whether you were on the mission or not, you could learn the same lessons that the team on the ground had learned. It also gave us a lot to talk about after a particularly interesting mission.

Ray's mission was a must-see. Ray's squadron had been in Afghanistan. His troop was assaulting a cluster of buildings behind a mud wall. Ray was one of the lead snipers and had climbed on top of a nearby building overlooking the compound where the Taliban commander was holed up, so that he could provide cover for the assaulters.

As I watched the footage, I could make out the assaulters moving silently toward the target compound. I had done the same thing a million times, so I knew exactly how those guys felt. I was still getting excited just watching them. I knew their senses were on fire, listening for an opening door or the crunch of stones under a pair of Taliban Cheetah sneakers. I caught myself scanning the walls of the compound looking for some movement.

As Ray set up to cover the assaulters, he took each step with care. I'm sure every creak of the thin mud roof gave him pause, knowing a wrong move would give away his position to people who could be sleeping in the house.

As the assault force closed in on the target, a door directly under Ray's position was thrown open from the inside. Then the distinct shape of an RPG—the thin tube with a cone-shaped warhead on the front—poked out. There was a brief pause, maybe a few seconds. I guessed someone inside Ray's building had heard him on the roof or had heard the assault-ers patrolling the compound. The Taliban fighter was proba-bly trying to make out the approaching SEALs in the dark. Seconds later, the rocket raced out, cutting a path right in front of the assaulters and detonating some distance away.

The shock wave from the backblast created by the RPG was powerful enough to cause the mud roof to collapse. The middle of the roof opened like a giant mouth and swallowed Ray, dropping him in the middle of the house.

Ray landed on a heap of broken wooden beams and mud. He immediately saw five Taliban fighters through the dust cloud, holding AK-47 assault rifles and wearing chest racks carrying extra magazines. A few were lying on the floor, stunned by the RPG's backblast.

Ray had only a few seconds to make a decision: stay in the room and shoot the five fighters or get out of the house before his fellow SEALs, who might not have seen him fall, opened fire on the building.

Ray decided to get out of the house.

He spotted a window and crashed through it. On the footage, I saw Ray fall out of the window in a heap, landing at the base of the wall. Ray yelled to his teammates, identifying himself as one of the good guys. He hoped his fellow assault-ers would realize he wasn't one of the Taliban. The footage showed Ray rolling away from the window and calmly pulling out a grenade. Crouching under the lip of the windowsill, he tossed the grenade into the house. From the drone feed, I thought Ray looked calm. All of his movements were smooth and fluid. He had a way of making something crazy look easy.

Ray rolled away from the open window and dove for some cover. The grenade exploded and sent a cloud of debris out of the hole in the roof. Inside the house, the shrapnel cut down the fighters.

Ray, like many of us, had served his country for more than a decade in some pretty hairy conditions. His actions reinforced the concepts we live by for the whole team, and I know that watching Ray operate at the peak of his ability made us more effective and saved lives down the line.

As I sat on my buddy's deck, I wished I'd had one more chance to have a beer with Ray. For the rest of the night, we talked about our fallen brothers and tried to forget everything else. It didn't matter how they died. It mattered only that they were gone.

Days later, details started to come in about the crash. It was important that we learned from it, like we did from Ray's mission. The lost guys had been part of a quick reaction force that night. The QRF is a standby unit, often waiting near a mission, that is ready to act as reinforcement at a moment's notice, if things turn bad.

Army Rangers had gone out to hit a target in Jaw-e-Mekh Zareen village in Wardak Province's Tangi Valley. The SEALs were originally offered the target but passed because illumination from the moon was high that night and they thought it would be safer to wait for darker conditions. But when the SEALs passed, the Rangers decided to hit the target instead.

They were after a senior Taliban leader. A firefight broke out almost as soon as the Rangers landed. Taliban fighters from up and down the valley came to defend the compound. The fight raged for at least two hours before a small group of Taliban started to flee. The Rangers called the QRF for help. They feared the group that had taken off included the commander and his bodyguards, and they didn't want to lose him.

As the helicopter—call sign Extortion Seventeen—came in to help the Rangers, an RPG from one of the Taliban fighters struck the aft rotor assembly. Ray and the guys didn't have a chance.

Two days later, commanders in Afghanistan claimed that the fighter who had fired the rocket-propelled grenade was killed by an F-16 bomb strike.

That didn't make it any easier.

Later, rumors about an elaborate trap started to circulate. There was talk that the Taliban had lured the SEALs to the target and shot down the helicopter in retaliation for the Osama bin Laden raid. But whatever the truth, the reality is that the downing of Extortion Seventeen was a tragedy. When the QRF is called in, it's almost always because something went wrong. Being the QRF is dangerous. There is no element of surprise, especially when you arrive in a CH-47 Chinook, which is essentially a flying school bus. Sometimes, there isn't enough skill or luck in the world when it is your time.

As the details rolled in that night, I knew a bunch more teammates had lost their lives in Afghanistan. Thirty-eight service members were killed when an RPG hit Extortion Seventeen. More than a dozen were SEALs. The crash was the deadliest day of the decade-long war in Afghanistan. The sight of the flag-draped caskets on the way to the memorial services is forever etched into my mind.

Of course, Ray isn't the only friend who was lost during my fourteen-year SEAL career. I have forty names in my cell phone contact list that I'll never call again. There have been many more than just forty SEALs killed since September 11, but these were the forty whom I was lucky enough to have known and served with.

We'll never relive the glory days of past deployments over a beer. No more cookouts or training trips. All forty guys are more than coworkers or friends. They are brothers. Every time I scroll through my contacts, I'll run across a name and instantly relive a memory.

We all arrived in San Diego with the same dream. It was a bond that put a kid from the backcountry of Alaska on the same page as a surfer from California and a pig farmer from the Midwest who saw the ocean for the first time on the first day of training.

I chased that dream from high school in Alaska to BUD/S. Once I got my trident, the iconic badge SEALs wear on their uniforms, I tried to excel at every task. For me, and for many of my teammates, being a SEAL was just the start of our dream. Being a great teammate, pushing to constantly improve, and being there for the guys to your left and right became a kind of religion for us.

I never became numb to the loss. For me it stung more and more as my career progressed. My teammates sacrificed everything for their country. They spent months away from family and loved ones, long hours suffering in the cold mountains of Afghanistan, and some, like my buddy Ray, paid the ultimate price. Not one of them thought of himself as a hero.

I was faced with a decision.

I'd spent fourteen years trying to be the best SEAL I could be. But now I either had to reenlist and stay in the Navy long enough to earn my pension—another six years—or get out and find a new challenge.

The decision weighed on me like nothing else in my life. Being a SEAL on one of the nation's premier ████████████ teams was more than just my job. It was my identity and one of the chief ways I brought order and meaning to my life. It wasn't like I could go overseas and run missions part-time. I knew once I left, the train was going to leave me far behind, and most of what I'd known my entire adult life would change forever.

As I wrestled with the decision, I spent nights examining my career and the events and lessons that came to define me. I ultimately decided to leave the Navy and forge a new path. In doing that, I had to reinvent myself.

The publication of the book thrust me into a world I had

never been in before, one where millions of people I had never met suddenly wanted to talk to me and hear what I had to say. Most of the people I met were supportive, but there was criticism as well. It was a new challenge, one that I couldn't be sure my SEAL training had prepared me for.

It took me thirteen deployments in thirteen years to become the operator I was when I left the Navy. Getting off the speeding train was difficult partly because I was heading into a world where I had no idea if my skills would apply.

When people hear about SEALs, they assume we're superheroes who jump out of airplanes and shoot bad guys. We do both those things, but those skills don't define us. When we make mistakes, we try again and again and again until we get it right. We're not superheroes. We're just committed.

There is no "secret sauce," but there is a lot of hard work, dedication, and drive.

The reality is that SEALs don't think of themselves as special. We simply strive to do the most basic tasks extraordinarily well. One of the best leaders I know used to challenge his junior guys to be engaged and part of the team.

"At what level are you willing to participate?" he'd ask.

"All in, all the time," was the only acceptable answer.

We've learned, often the hard way, how to excel. Excelling means communicating with each other, testing, leading, listening, studying, and teaching, day after day, year after year. It means not just being able to trek miles through the mountains of Afghanistan carrying sixty pounds on your back, but also letting others call you out on your mistakes. And getting called out by your teammates is often harder than spending hours in the cold surf.

As I faced new challenges in my first year outside the Navy, I spent a lot of time going back to the lessons I learned during my SEAL career, and the moments and people whom I know I will carry with me the rest of my life. What I realized is that the important moments for me are not the moments that made headlines back home. They are the missions that have no name, in which my team was tested and learned something that made us better. They are the mistakes I made that I thankfully survived and learned from so I wouldn't make the same mistake the next time. The most important moments are the ones that taught me what the SEAL brotherhood really means.

This book is about those moments, and the lessons from each one that define me.

Taken together, I hope these stories provide an intimate glimpse into the life and work of a SEAL and the lessons passed down to me by the teammates I served with and those who came before me.

Being a SEAL is not just a job. It is a lifelong commitment to challenge yourself, and your teammates, to exist in a constant state of evolution, examining your decisions and learning from your mistakes so that you and your team can be as effective as possible.

The lessons I learned over my career make up the legacy of the men, like Ray, we lost and all the other active and former SEALs who have dedicated their lives to this country. Many were learned the hard way, through the sacrifice of friends. This book is dedicated to my brothers.

SEALs are taught to mentor the younger generation and to pass the lessons we've learned on to the newer guys. I wrote *No Hero* because that is what I plan to do.

CHAPTER I

The Right to Wear the Shirt

Purpose

It was just a black T-shirt.

Size medium, one hundred percent cotton.

On the front was a skeleton in a wetsuit crawling over the beach. He had an M-16 in his hands and a knife on his belt. The skeleton was coming out of the surf, the dark waves crashing behind him. A SEAL trident was on the left breast of the T-shirt. The trident was the sole reason I got the T-shirt in the first place.

I remember when it came in the mail. There was no way I could get a shirt like this from a store in the Alaskan village where I grew up. I put it on as soon as I opened it, and wore it practically every day. If that shirt was clean in the morning, I was wearing it.

To everyone else, it was just a shirt I always wore. But to me, it represented my goal in life. Each time I wore it, the shirt renewed my quest to become a SEAL. I slid the shirt into my suitcase and finished packing the rest of my clothes—including a borrowed suit and dress shoes—and headed for the airstrip. I was on my way to a conference in Washington, D.C., for "future military members." It was 1992, and to this day I don't know how I got invited, but it probably came from one of the many recruiters I'd talked with about being a SEAL.

The airstrip was on the outskirts of the village, and it was our only lifeline to "civilization," if you can call any town in Alaska that. The frontier lifestyle is why people move to Alaska. If you want convenience, stay in the lower forty-eight.

I watched the bush plane clear the trees at the far end of the strip and come in for a landing. As the pilot and a newly arrived group of hunters unloaded, I hugged my parents near the small one-room building that served as the airport terminal.

The trip was a first for me. It was the first time I'd left Alaska alone. It was my first trip to Washington, D.C. But of all the firsts, I was most excited that I was going to meet my first SEAL.

Everyone in my village in Alaska knew I wanted to be a SEAL. It was something I talked about with my friends and dreamed about at night. I read every book I could find on the SEALs.

I knew nothing of SEAL Team ▓ until I read *Rogue Warrior* by Richard Marcinko. "Demo Dick" and "Shark Man of the Delta" were some of his nicknames. He operated in Vietnam and later started SEAL Team ▓. *Rogue Warrior* tells the story of the creation of the unit. If you believe that book, every SEAL can bench-press five hundred pounds and eat glass. I wanted more than anything to prove I could too. Except for maybe eating glass.

At the time, I just thought it would be cool to be a SEAL.

I knew the training would be hard, but I was too young to really understand how hard. I certainly didn't know all of the sacrifices I would have to make. I just wanted to be like the guys I read about, and at the time that was enough to push me forward.

I was lucky. I figured out my purpose early on. I don't think I understood it at first, but from the moment I found out about SEALs, I knew that was my goal, because of the challenge. If you asked me then to say *why* I wanted to join, a sense of duty would be on the list, but not at the top. At the top was a need to prove to myself I could make it through the toughest training the U.S. military had to offer. Why would I want to do something that was easy? If it were easy, everybody would do it. Looking back now, I'm not sure why I had to prove myself. All I knew was after reading the history books, I decided the SEALs always stood out as the hardest and most challenging. I guess I figured if I was going to join the military, I might as well go big.

The pilot helped me stow my suitcase and I climbed aboard the plane. I waved to my parents from my cramped seat in the back as we taxied into position on the runway. My family wasn't rich, but my parents offered to cover the airplane ticket, and two Army veterans from the village covered the remaining costs.

At the airport in Anchorage, I pulled the itinerary for the trip out and went over it again. Before the SEAL session, I'd have to endure trips to the national monuments and listen to sessions on the Army and Air Force.

But it was worth it to meet a SEAL.

I got to Washington and instantly fell into the rhythm of the conference. We went to the Pentagon, which is much cooler in the movies. It is really just an odd-shaped office building. We also saw the Lincoln and Vietnam Memorials. At the time, nothing held my interest. The vast number of names on the Vietnam Memorial took me aback, but the impact faded because I hadn't experienced loss like I would years later in Iraq and Afghanistan. Thinking back now, I really had no idea that someday I'd look at a list of names like the wall and understand just what it means to lose close friends and teammates. Visiting the wall now, I understand the gravity. But at that time, I was just fixated on meeting the SEAL.

Everything was scheduled to the minute, and each morning as I pulled on my clothes I saw my T-shirt still neatly folded. I was saving it for the SEAL session.

The session was in the afternoon, so after the typical sandwich-and-cookie conference lunch, I hurried over to the meeting room where the SEAL was going to speak. Unfortunately, when I got to the door, they said the room was full.

The room was jammed with people, but I could still see a few chairs. I tried to reason with the woman guarding the door. She was one of the chaperones and organizers who were with us throughout the week. I could tell she wanted to let me in, but there were only a set number of seats.

She was apologetic but didn't budge.

There was a small crowd gathering outside. The SEAL session was the hallmark of the period. Through the door, I could see the SEAL in his uniform talking with the younger chaperones. Time was running out. I opened my itinerary, looking at the other sessions, but nothing came close. I didn't know what to do. I'd flown more than four thousand miles to attend this session. At that moment, the whole trip was wasted. I was crushed.

Then, just before the session was about to begin, the lady at the door waved me over to her. She told me they were going to let a few more people go in and ushered me inside. It was standing-room only. I found a spot in the back and waited for the SEAL to begin.

The SEAL was wearing a green BDU camouflage uniform with a black balaclava pulled down around his neck. His pants were tucked into black-and-green jungle boots. He had longer hair than you'd expect for someone in the military. Not shaggy, but not the high-and-tight haircut favored by the Marines. He had an air of cockiness about him, a fact I realized years later. More cocky than confident, he lacked the self-awareness to know that it wasn't cool to act cool.

His session started with the SEAL boilerplate stuff. SEALs are the Navy's primary special operations force. The acronym SEAL comes from the unit's ability to operate at sea, in the air, and on land. President John F. Kennedy saw a need for special operations forces to fight guerrilla wars and created the SEALs with the Army's Special Forces. In his 1961 speech announcing plans to land a man on the moon, Kennedy also laid out plans to invest one hundred million dollars to create and train special operations forces.

Populated at first by members of the Navy's underwater demolition teams, SEALs were deployed to Vietnam, where they worked with the CIA and set up ambushes to slow the supply lines in the Mekong Delta. SEALs earned the nickname "men with green faces" because of the camouflage face paint they often wore on missions.

I hung on each word for the hour-long presentation. He told stories about Basic Underwater Demolition/SEALs or BUD/S training. He stressed how tough it was; nothing about BUD/S was easy, from the frigid swims in the ocean to the grueling runs in the soft beach sand. His stories just made me want it more.

After the question-and-answer period, we had a short break before the next event. I ran upstairs to my hotel room to change into my black SEAL T-shirt. I wanted to get my picture taken with the SEAL. I figured if I was going to get a photo, I'd better be wearing my favorite shirt. When I got back to the room, the SEAL was still talking and taking questions.

I waited patiently for my turn.

"Hey, can I get a picture with you?" I asked, shaking his hand.

He smiled and put an arm over my shoulder. If he told me to shave my head and walk backward the rest of the week, I'd have done it. Just before one of the chaperones snapped the picture, he leaned over and whispered into my ear.

"Hey, you know you usually get your ass kicked for wearing a SEAL T-shirt when you're not a SEAL," he said.

I smiled and thanked him, but at that moment all I wanted to do was get the shirt off. I raced up to my hotel room and buried the shirt in the bottom of my suitcase. I never put it on again. When I got home, I put it in the back of my dresser drawer. I wasn't a poseur. I just hadn't had a chance to prove myself yet. The comment didn't sting as much as it fueled my passion to actually become a SEAL. I felt like I'd cheated myself by wearing it. It was then I realized my desire to be a SEAL wasn't an adolescent fantasy. It was the only thing in my mind that would give my life some real meaning and purpose. I wanted to earn the right to wear the shirt.

Once I realized my purpose was to be a SEAL, I never stopped trying to achieve it. Looking back, I think my parents taught me that having a purpose and living up to it was important. My parents were young when their purpose brought them to Alaska, and I knew it meant sacrifice and hardship.

My parents were missionaries. Their faith drove them to move our family from California to Alaska, far from any of the creature comforts of a city. There was nothing easy about living in a village, but that didn't matter to my parents. Everyone was poor by suburban American standards, but really it was just a more simple life.

We lived in a two-story house one hundred yards off a river. I saw moose from my front door so often that it didn't amaze me. There was one TV station and no radio. Our house had water and electricity, but no central heating. We used a massive iron stove in the living room to keep warm in the winter. My father would get up in the middle of the night to make sure the fire was still going.

A huge hopper stood next to the stove. It was my job to keep it full of wood in the winter. I'd split the logs and keep the woodpile stacked on the porch. As the stack in the hopper dwindled, I'd be out on the porch getting another load. Chores for me weren't a way to make some spending money. We never got paid. It was part of my family's team effort to survive in Alaska.

One of my first memories of elementary school was fire building. Instead of just teaching us how to read or write, our school taught us survival skills. Each student in my third-grade class got two matches to start a survival fire using bark from trees surrounding the school. We had to build a fire big enough to stay warm during a winter day. The drill was designed to teach us the survival skills that we might need if we ever got lost or became stranded. Alaska's wilderness can be a very dangerous place if you don't know what you're doing, making the walk to and from school hazardous.

My high school was one hallway with six rooms. It had about seventy kids in grades seven through twelve. My senior class was three students. I graduated as the valedictorian; just don't ask me what my grade point average was. My interests were mostly outside the classroom.

I hunted as often as I could. When I was a teenager my father would let me take the family boat up the river for long camping and hunting trips. I wanted to be outside and active, which likely led to my goal of being a SEAL. I never wanted to have to deal with stoplights, traffic, and wearing a suit to work every day. The thought of working in a cubicle sounded like a death sentence.

I purchased my first assault rifle at school from my history teacher. It was an AR-15, a civilian version of the military's M-4. I'd earned the money for the rifle doing odd jobs for people in the village and working construction in the summer. Between classes, I paid my teacher seven hundred dollars, then took the rifle and locked it in my locker until the end of school. When the bell rang, I put it on the back of my snowmobile and rode home. Yes, I did ride a snowmobile to school in the winter.

Anything we couldn't get from the land, we bought from the two stores in town, or during a semiannual trip to Anchorage to stock up. Because we lived so far from Anchorage, groceries were expensive. Milk was six dollars a gallon in the village, so my parents bought less expensive powdered milk.

The powdered milk was sold in massive tubs, too big to store on the kitchen counter. To make it easier for daily use, my mother measured out small amounts and put the powdered milk in plastic bags. She did the same thing with the tub of laundry soap and other bulk goods.

One morning, I fixed myself a big bowl of cereal. My mother was busy at the stove making pancakes for my father. The batter was bubbling up into big, fluffy pancakes as I poured the milk over my cereal.

Sitting at the table, I took a few bites, but it didn't taste right. I stirred the cereal around and I swore I saw suds. I started to get up to throw the bowl of cereal away, when my father stopped me.

"Eat it," he said. "It's just the powdered milk, and that is the way it tastes."

I tried to protest. "It isn't that," I said. "It has a sour taste. It tastes like soap."

"You just have to get used to it," my father said.

I never liked the taste of powdered milk, but there was something wrong with this batch. I choked down the whole bowl one spoonful at a time. After a while, my taste buds died. I couldn't taste anything but the sour, soapy flavor of the milk. My father's pancakes showed up soon after I finished my cereal. He took one bite and spit it out.

"What is wrong with these?" he asked my mother.

My mom stopped plating a short stack of pancakes for my sister and gave the batter a quick stir. She then picked up the plastic bag and sniffed it.

"I think I might have used laundry detergent instead of powdered milk," she said, with a sheepish smirk on her face. "No wonder the pancakes bubbled up so much."

My mother started to laugh, then my father. When they realized I'd eaten a bowl of cereal with soapy water, they laughed harder. I tried to laugh too, until my stomach started to hurt.

My mother poured out the batter and started fresh. When she offered me a fresh bowl of cereal, I declined. My stomach was doing flips and I had bubble guts the rest of the day.

Living in Alaska was hard, and it wasn't always because I

had liquid soap in my cereal. There was nothing normal about my upbringing, but my parents knew the sacrifices they were making. They didn't have to choke down horrible-tasting powdered milk or live in a village deep in the Alaskan wilderness. They chose to live a harder life than most because it was the only way my parents could achieve their purpose in life, to be missionaries and spread their faith. I know their dedication rubbed off on me. It gave me the values I needed to eventually excel in the Navy.

My parents set me on a course that wasn't the norm in the village. People didn't leave the village. They found jobs working construction in the summer and just lived off their savings and the land during the winter. My parents urged me to dream big and find my own way. I was one of the few kids I grew up with who had plans of doing something beyond staying in the village.

My father was always fair and never pushed me to do anything beyond what he knew I could accomplish. So when he asked me to at least try one year of college before enlisting in the Navy, I had to honor his wish. He was part of the Vietnam generation and didn't want anything to happen to me, but I think he also understood my passion to serve because he'd felt the same passion for his missionary work.

So we made a deal.

After high school graduation, I enrolled at a small college in Southern California and made a commitment to stay for at least a year. But I didn't plan on being there a day longer than that. After the first year, I planned to enlist and go to BUD/S.

My first year flew by, and my father was right. College was fun. Experiencing life outside of the village was actually pretty cool. My grade point average wasn't setting any records, but I was having a great time and making new friends. I'd promised him one year, but I decided to stick it out and finish my degree.

My school didn't have a Navy Reserve Officers' Training Corps (ROTC) program, and the surrounding programs didn't have a partnership agreement. The Army program at Cal State Fullerton did accept students from neighboring schools, so I signed up.

ROTC is a college-based program for training officers. Students take military science courses, work out, and drill together. Once a week typically, ROTC students wear uniforms to school. I'd take classes at my school during the day, and then drive across town for events and military science classes at Cal State. My goal wasn't to become an officer or join the Army. I just wanted to be involved in something military. I liked wearing the uniform; it gave me a sense of pride.

After my freshman year, the ROTC instructors asked if I wanted to go to the United States Army Airborne School at Fort Benning, Georgia. I'd excelled in my first semester, and they figured this carrot would not only keep me in the program, but also convince me to take a scholarship and be a future Army officer.

I accepted the chance to go to jump school, which is what most people call the airborne training program. I'd read enough books to know the SEALs sent guys straight from

BUD/S to get airborne qualified. I figured this was a chance to knock out the three-week school early. Before I left, I got a short haircut like the rest of my classmates.

The first morning, we got up at dawn and lined up in formation on the parade field near our barracks. The sun was just peeking over the pine trees, and the air was already humid and sticky. By the second exercise, my gray Army T-shirt was soaked.

Everyone looked the same—gray shirts, black shorts, high-and-tight haircuts—except for a small group of guys who had longer hair and brown T-shirts. When I saw the group in their uniforms after physical training, I noticed they had U.S. Navy name tapes over their left pockets. I knew they had to be SEALs.

The SEALs stuck together during training. I watched as the instructors corrected a SEAL and ordered him to do ten push-ups as punishment. As soon as the SEAL started, his buddies hit the floor too. In unison, they called out the reps. "One, two, three . . ." No one approached them, even though I desperately wanted to pick their brains about BUD/S.

If I'm being honest, I wanted to *be* them.

During the second week of training, I finally got to talk with one of the SEALs. It was lunch and the only seat open was across from me. We didn't talk at first, except for a nod. I was too intimidated to initiate a conversation. But after a few bites of his lunch, the SEAL finally spoke.

"Hey, bro, can I ask you a question?" he asked.

Unlike the SEAL I met in Washington, this one was skinnier, with shorter hair. He was lean and had an air of confidence, not arrogance.

"Sure," I said.

It was kind of exciting to finally be talking to one of the SEALs. In the back of my head, I wanted to be the one asking questions. I had so many, especially since I knew he'd just finished training. But while I saw my future, the SEAL just saw another cadet playing Army for three weeks.

"What is up with the haircuts?" the SEAL said. "I just don't get it. Why do you have that haircut?"

I stopped eating.

I couldn't believe this question was directed to me. The question wasn't asked to be mean or mocking. It felt like he was really curious, which made it worse. If he'd mocked me, I'd at least have been justified in being mad.

"I don't know, man," I said. "I really don't know."

I quickly tried to change the subject to BUD/S. I really didn't want to be talking about something I didn't truly understand. And I felt uncomfortable, embarrassed really.

Before the end of the conversation, I made up my mind. I was done with the Army. I went back to California and turned in my uniforms and boots, no longer shined to a high gloss. My high-and-tight haircut was starting to grow out.

As I finished up the paperwork, one of the officers at the unit stopped me.

"Hey, man, are you sure you want to leave?" the officer said. "We need good cadets and would hate to see you go."

"I just can't do this," I finally said.

The instructor tried to reason with me.

"You're a great cadet," he said. "We only send the top cadets to jump school."

I appreciated the compliment, but I didn't want to be in the Army.

"I want to be a SEAL," I said. "It has been my dream since I was a kid."

I knew I was taking a risk. By leaving ROTC, I was giving up the chance of a scholarship. But it was worth it, and I think sometimes you can achieve a goal only if you are willing to risk it all. Take my parents moving out to Alaska, far from family and any support, to achieve their goals. This was no longer some idea I had because I thought it was cool. It had become the beacon that was driving my life decisions.

I'm confident many of the guys who became my teammates were the same. We all wanted to be part of something bigger. I'd veered off my path and lost focus on what I really wanted.

When I finally signed my Navy enlistment contract, I had to pick an "A" school, which was basically deciding which job I'd perform if I washed out of BUD/S and didn't become a SEAL. The recruiter wanted me to go into nuclear power, or "nuke," to work on the reactors that propelled the subs and aircraft carriers. The school took eighteen months. I knew recruiters probably got a bonus for putting people in the toughest programs, but I didn't want to wait that long to start BUD/S.

"What is the shortest school available?" I asked the recruiter.

He flipped through his files and found a chart with details on all the schools. Running his finger down the list, he stopped and looked up at me.

"Torpedoman. Seven weeks," the recruiter said, resigned to the fact he wasn't going to get me to go nuke and boost his numbers.

Instead, I'd be waxing torpedoes for a couple months before hopefully getting a chance to go to BUD/S. I didn't spend a lot of time thinking about what would happen if I washed out. Four years as a torpedoman would have driven me crazy, and maybe out of the Navy altogether. For me at that time, there was no backup plan.

I set my goals higher than most people thought were possible for a kid from Alaska, but I knew in my guts that I'd make it or die trying. I didn't want to be an old man and regret not trying.

There was some comfort in finally working toward my ultimate goal of becoming a SEAL. I'd learned sacrifice from my parents. They showed me what it meant to live for something bigger than myself. I got off track when I signed up for ROTC. It took that lunch at jump school to push me back on track. When I looked in the mirror, I saw someone with the drive and discipline to make it happen. I saw someone with a purpose. I just needed a chance to prove I was up to it. I knew nothing in my life would feel right unless I at least gave it my best shot.

"Seven weeks," I said. "Sign me up."

CHAPTER 2

How to Swim Fifty Meters Underwater Without Dying

Confidence

Ice floated in the water outside of my hotel window as I zipped my dry suit shut.

I'd been staring out of the window off and on since we'd spotted the bloody sea lion carcass on the shore that morning. The sea lion's body had a huge gash in its side, and the ice around it was bloodred. A killer whale did it, or that is what the locals told us. I would have appreciated the scene more, but in less than an hour, my SEAL teammates and I were about to get in the same water to plant a bomb on a U.S. Navy ship.

I took some solace in the fact that at least the killer whale had a full stomach.

I was a brand-new SEAL, having graduated BUD/S just nine months earlier, and it was cool to be back in Alaska training. The scenario was pretty simple. My SEAL platoon got tapped to play the OPFOR—military jargon for "opposing force," or the bad guys. It was our job to attack an amphibious assault ship moored at the pier in Ketchikan, Alaska. We had to sneak in close enough to the ship to set tracking devices. Some of the ship's crew as well as a small contingent of Army soldiers would be guarding the ship and surrounding areas. Their task was to defend against a threat like us.

There was a foot of snow on the pier and the water temperature was hovering just above freezing as we prepared. I smeared black paint on my face and squeezed all of my warm clothes under my dry suit.

One of my teammates knocked on my door, and I grabbed the rest of my gear and headed out. We met in the parking lot of our hotel and the four of us on the OPFOR assault team—all dressed in dry suits and painted faces—climbed into the back of a U-Haul truck. We were the brand-new guys in the platoon.

If the dark, cold water and the seal-eating killer whales weren't scary enough, we also had to worry about Flipper, a killer dolphin stalking us from the deep.

I'm not kidding.

The Navy has bottlenose dolphins trained to attack divers. The dolphins were part of the U.S. Navy Marine Mammal Program, which trained both dolphins and sea lions to detect mines and protect harbors and ships. Both the United States and Russia spent millions on these kinds of training programs, and the dolphins were used in combat during the Gulf War and in operations off the coast of Iraq. The Russian program was disbanded in the late 1990s, and word was their killer dolphins were sold to Iran.

The Navy had flown three dolphins up to Alaska from San Diego in heated tanks so that they could hunt us. One dolphin was stationed in a cage at each end of the ship that was our target, and the third was free-swimming. The dolphins in the cages were trained to use their sonar to detect divers. When they heard us coming, the dolphins were supposed to surface and ring a bell attached to the cage. The dolphin handlers would then call in via radio that the dolphin had heard something, and the patrol boats would come looking for us.

When the free-swimming dolphin spotted a swimmer, it attacked, forcing the diver to the surface. We had to deal with a giant dolphin swimming full speed in the dark water repeatedly bashing us with its nose until we swam to the surface. It's no fun heading into icy, pitch-black water in the dead of night under any conditions, but the constant possibility of a giant dolphin ramming you at full speed added a little anxiety to the mission.

A few hours before we hit the water, two of my teammates in plain clothes had made their way along a nearby dock with a pair of dive tanks. When they got near the ship, they opened the valves at the top of the tanks, allowing just enough air to escape to make bubbles. My teammates tied the tanks together and dropped them over the side of the pier, lashing the anchor line to the rail before they walked away. The bubbles were white noise underwater to cover our approach.

With the tanks in the water, we left the hotel and headed toward the river that ran from the town to the channel. We bounced along the rutted roads of Ketchikan in the back of the U-Haul. I could hear our equipment rattle as tanks banged against the wall. No one spoke. I was nervous. I wasn't the best swimmer, and navigating underwater in pitch-black darkness while hunted by a killer dolphin wasn't going to be easy. But it wasn't the dolphins or the killer whale that scared me the most. It was the swim to the ship.

Much of the town was built on a wooden dock where the ship was moored. The conventional approach would have been to swim out in the main channel, which is where the dolphins were stationed. We had decided to sneak in from under the immense pier network. If we came in from the river, the large stanchions holding the pier together would mask our movement. But that also meant we'd be swimming in complete darkness through a maze of pylons and debris. We couldn't use flashlights for fear of attracting the dolphins below or the guards patrolling the dock above us. We would have to silently feel our way from pylon to pylon. This swim was going to be all by touch, as we worked our way through the water.

The truck coasted to a stop and we could hear the driver— another teammate—talking to a security guard. My heart rate kicked up and we held our collective breath. If they searched the truck, the mission was done. We sat for only a few seconds, likely because of traffic backed up at the check-point, but it was a very long few seconds. At last I could hear the engine roar as we headed to the bank of the creek.

I felt the truck slow and then stop. The driver cut the engine and seconds later threw open the back door. I climbed out of the truck with the other three divers and trudged through the snow to the water.

We got into pairs and attached a line to each other so no one would get lost. I would never be more than four feet apart from my swim buddy. We waded into the water. I took two long and slow deep breaths, put in my regulator, and slipped into the creek. With our goggles on and dive rigs ready to go, we gave each other a quick thumbs-up and began submerging ourselves in the frigid water. I had to stifle a gasp as the ice-cold water washed over my head and face. In seconds it was pitch-black.

"I hate diving," I thought.

I was nervous. This was one of my first missions—it was training, but we were in an uncontrolled environment and the dangers were real—and I wasn't completely comfortable in the water. I knew being a SEAL meant underwater operations, but I dreaded them. The water portion of BUD/S was hard for me. The long runs and push-ups during BUD/S never worried me, but the water tests did. I wasn't a surfer. I wasn't really a swimmer. I had never done a lot of swimming as a kid in Alaska.

I can remember my dad challenged me once when I was almost a teenager to swim across the river in front of our house. The current pushed against me as I slowly swam. By the time I reached the far bank, I was a quarter of a mile downriver from where I'd started. That was the farthest I'd swum before I started training for BUD/S. When it came time to pass the fifty-meter underwater swim during BUD/S, I had the same nervous feeling as I had getting ready to dive under the dock in Alaska.

The fifty-meter underwater swim is one of the first pass-or-fail tests during BUD/S. I remember it was a sunny day in June, the clouds having burned away to reveal a blue sky. The pool was across from the BUD/S training area on Naval Base Coronado, which sits across the bay from San Diego.

My BUD/S class ran over to the pool in the morning. We'd already spent hours in the cold surf doing flutter kicks and running for miles in the sand. We all knew the test was coming, and there was a nervous energy up and down the ranks. We crowded on one side of the pool in our tan shorts, shirtless and barefoot, and listened to the safety brief.

"If you want to stay in this training, you're going to have to do this swim," the instructor told us as we huddled on the deck. "The key is to stay as relaxed as you can."

The swim wasn't timed. Swim fifty meters in the twelve-foot-deep pool—down and back in one breath. Safety swimmers were positioned above and below us as we swam. Doctors and an ambulance waited poolside in case of emergency.

The test was simple, on paper. But that was before the instructors took away any advantages. No diving off the wall. We had to step out far enough to do a front flip underwater, so once you started toward the far end of the pool you had no forward momentum.

The underwater swim was part of the first phase of BUD/S, which includes a grueling five-and-a-half-day stretch called Hell Week. During Hell Week, each candidate sleeps only about four total hours but runs more than two hundred miles and does physical training for more than twenty hours per day.

BUD/S is all about training your mind and body to achieve more than you think possible. It is the first test in a SEAL's training and career. The SEAL motto, "The only easy day was yesterday," was about to become very clear to us.

I don't think I realized it at the time, but BUD/S is a series of building blocks starting with the fifty-meter swim and Hell Week in the first phase, followed by dive training in the second phase, and then firearms and explosives training in the final phase. Basically, you start with baby steps and end up doing the things that can kill you if not handled correctly. You have to pass each one to keep going. Fail once and you wash out.

I knew, coming from Alaska, that swimming was going to be my weakest skill. My SEAL buddy in college taught me the breaststroke and the sidestroke, which is all I needed. And for one semester, I worked out with my college club team. But of all the tests in BUD/S, this one worried me. I knew it was all or nothing. I knew no matter how tired, nervous, or scared I was, I couldn't let doubt creep into my head. I had to make it.

After the safety briefing, we sat in lines—nut to butt, as we say—in our tan shorts. Over my shoulder, I could hear splashes as my classmates jumped into the pool. The night before, guys had been full of tips and advice. We'd talked about trying to stay deep. I didn't want to be a foot underwater, because I might be tempted to poke my head up. I had decided to try to stay at six or seven feet.

There was no talking as I waited for my name to be called. A few minutes before I stepped to the edge of the pool, I took two deep breaths. I wanted to slow everything down in my mind in an attempt to relax and focus.

"This is easy," I told myself as I walked to the edge of the pool. "All the instructors did it. It's not impossible. Chill out."

When it was my turn to go, I stepped feetfirst into the pool and disappeared under the surface. I pushed my head down and kicked my legs over into a flip. I could feel the water surge up my nose, forcing me to blow out some of my last breath. I was uncomfortable from the start.

I pushed my hands up and using the breaststroke started toward the far end of the pool. It looked more than twenty-five meters away. I knew the test was a battle of distance, not time. I didn't hurry. Instead, I concentrated on slow, deliberate strokes. There is a saying, "Slow is smooth and smooth is fast." I was living proof as I glided below the surface.

I felt good physically, but I couldn't stop my mind from thinking about how far away the wall looked. At the bottom of the pool, I spotted one of the instructors. He had a regulator in his mouth connected to a scuba tank. I watched as he tracked us from the bottom, ready to spring up and rescue one of us if we started to drown.

Above me, another instructor with a scuba mask and snorkel kept pace. He looked like a predator ready to dive after his prey.

The whole swim takes only forty seconds to a minute, but it felt a lot longer. My lungs kept reminding me I needed air and my mind was begging me to surface. As I reached the wall, I spun around and set my legs to push with all my might.

It felt good to have some momentum heading back to where I started.

By now, the burning in my lungs was impossible to ignore. I knew I'd be "chicken necking" soon. That is the first step before you pass out. Think of it as a gag reflex. I could feel my head start to bob as my body tried to force me to breathe. The first feelings of panic started to tingle, but I quickly pushed them deeper into my mind. Instead, I focused on my slow, deliberate stroke, as the wall grew larger and larger.

"Just keep swimming," I pleaded with myself. "Keep swimming."

But I couldn't stop the gasping. It wasn't mental. It was my body in revolt. My lungs were on fire, threatening to come out of my chest. My mind started to panic and my focus began to wane. It isn't natural to deny your body air. We're hardwired to survive, and we need air to do it.

But I fought to get control of my mind. I focused on the ever-growing far wall. I committed to staying underwater. I refused to give up. This was the first real test. If I couldn't do this in a clean, heated pool in sunny San Diego, what was I going to do in the North Atlantic during a storm?

The chicken necking eventually stopped, and with each stroke, I got closer to the wall. But I could also feel myself losing consciousness. My vision blurred around the edges. With each stroke, the darkness started to crowd my vision. Like a fog, the shadow started in my peripheral vision and I knew in a few seconds I might pass out.

I had to be near the wall. I reached out to touch it. Rough hands grabbed me under my arms. The instructors pulled me out of the water like a trophy fish. I flopped down on the pool deck and took a deep breath. I could feel my lungs draw in deep, and my body relaxed. I took several more deep breaths and then tried to get up.

"Stay down," I heard one of the instructors bark at me.

I rested my head back on the warm deck. It's rare for instructors in BUD/S to let you rest, and I was going to take full advantage. One by one my classmates finished. I watched the instructors throw the limp body of one of my classmates up onto the deck. He was out cold. After a few quick breaths, he gagged and coughed his way back to consciousness. The minute he did, he looked at the nearest instructor.

"Did I make it?"

The fact that seconds before, he was unconscious seemed like a minor detail. I understood because, like him, I didn't want to fail. Failure was almost worse than death.

"Stay down," an instructor said. "Relax."

I was enjoying the sun on my back. It was paradise, for a few seconds. The instructors saw I was fine.

"Get the fuck up and head over to the pass line. You did it." Those were great words to hear.

No one who makes it through BUD/S ever thought he'd fail. BUD/S is relentless and forced me to dig deep. I never doubted myself. I knew I'd pass. I think people mistake a SEAL's confidence for arrogance. But after the fifty-meter swim, Hell Week, and dive training, where the instructors do their best to drown you, we know our limits and we know how to push well beyond them. During BUD/S I overcame dozens of obstacles that looked insurmountable at the time, and that gave me the confidence to know I could do it again.

But bobbing in the near-freezing river in Alaska, I had to work hard to muster that confidence. I wasn't sure I could do this, but tied to my buddy and nearing the opening to the pier, I didn't have a lot of choice.

It took only a few minutes before I couldn't feel my face. We let the current push us toward the harbor. At its widest the Ketchikan Creek is only about twenty feet and only five feet deep, so we bobbed at the surface until we crossed the first bridge. We were using Draeger diving rigs, which use pure oxygen. There are no bubbles when we exhale, keeping us much quieter.

As we passed under the bridge, I could hear the snow crunching under the tires of the cars above. Somewhere above us, I knew guards patrolled. Spotlights from the ship criss-crossed the black water, looking for us.

The water got deeper under the bridge, and before we crossed underneath we dipped below the surface. It was difficult to see anything in the ink-black water. We swam to the right bank and started searching for an opening in the pylons that led under the pier.

I could feel the tug of the rope on my belt as my partner swam nearby. I found the edge of the first pylon, figured out the direction I needed to move, and plunged farther into the darkness. I held my hand out in front and slowly kicked my way past the first pylon. My hand brushed against it, sinking into the green algae clinging to the wood.

Any minute, I expected to be pummeled by the dolphin's nose as it forced me to the surface. We crept more than swam as we picked our way through the maze of algae-covered pylons.

Debris littered the bottom. Several times my flippers brushed against metal or trash. Each time we got close to a pylon, we had to be careful of jagged nails. If we tore a hole in our dry suit it would be more than just cold; it could be fatal because water would fill the suit, making it impossible to surface. Drowning was a real possibility.

I knew my swim buddy was near because of the tension in the rope. It was so dark that I remember lifting my hand and putting it directly in front of my face. I couldn't see anything. Besides the dark, we had to deal with the cold. Beyond the cold we had to worry about the dolphins, and besides the dolphins we had to worry about getting lost under a town built on pylons. It felt claustrophobic.

I could barely make out the reading on the glowing green compass on my wrist. I tried to keep a steady pace on the right heading, but every few feet I had to dodge around a pylon. It took us an hour to get to the ship. I was relieved when we finally reached the ship's hull. It's surprising when you're swimming in the pitch black with your hands in front of you and you swim into the massive hull of a warship. It makes you feel so small. I quickly snapped out of congratulating myself for making it when I realized we were only half done. In order to complete the mission, we had to place the device and make it back to our truck without being detected.

From below the water line, the ship was massive. I ran my gloved hand over the rough steel and waited for my partner to remove the collapsible pole strapped to my back. The pole was like the one used to replace letters on a sign at a gas station. The head of the pole had magnets and rollers on it. I pulled one of two dummy bomb devices out of a bag on my belt and attached it to the head. I ran my hand over the wheels on the head to make sure they rolled freely and tapped my partner on the shoulder. He placed the rollers on the skin of the ship and slowly slid the training device up the side, letting it roll along the hull until it was in place. The device attached to the ship by magnets. As it broke the water line, we got the device's magnets too close to the skin of the ship. I felt the device grab hold of the hull of the ship with a "thunk." I pushed the pole back and forth until the bomb came free. I worried the noise of the magnet pulling the device toward the ship had given away our position.

I closed my eyes and tried to focus. I was doing it all by feel only. I couldn't see anything anyway, and my mind was playing tricks on me. I kept seeing movement in the black water. Each time, my heart raced, waiting to feel a dolphin or killer whale barreling into my side at full speed.

Inch by inch we slid the device up the hull of the ship until it reached the three-foot line.

After we got the second device in place, my partner helped me collapse the pole. He lashed it in place on my back and we started the long, cold swim back to where the truck had dropped us off. It was a total relief when we swam back under the bridge. This time, there were fewer cars passing along the bridge and from a light posted by the road I could make out that it had begun to snow again. I was tired and my nerves were frazzled after working in complete darkness for well over two hours. But in my head I knew the only relief was up the creek and into the back of a U-Haul truck.

My legs shook when I stood up onshore. Someone threw a blanket over me and helped me drag my gear to the truck. I could barely talk because my face was still numb. Minutes later I was back in the dark as the truck rumbled back to the hotel. I couldn't feel my face, but I know I had a smile.

We were a bunch of new guys fresh from BUD/S and we'd just completed the mission. It was a training mission, but diving under the pier wasn't easy. We'd been on other training missions before, but this time our officer trusted us to plan and execute the mission on our own and we succeeded. It felt good to be trusted.

"Anybody see the dolphin?" a teammate said.

"Nope," I said. "I couldn't see shit."

"Every time I felt the water move, I tensed up, ready to get the shit beat out of me," my partner said.

It turns out the free-swimming dolphin had spotted the smorgasbord of fish in the harbor and taken off. The two dolphins in the cages—used to the warmer San Diego Bay—stayed near the surface and every ten minutes rang the bell to get a fish. The dolphins didn't want to be in the cold water any more than we did. The steady noise from the tanks masked our approach from the dolphins, and nobody had seen or heard us plant the training devices. We had actually pulled off the mission.

I was nervous the entire time. But I used the exact same focus to get through this mission as I did the fifty-meter underwater swim back in BUD/S. My confidence was growing, but it wasn't a hundred percent yet. When I got into combat a few years later, I couldn't focus on the negative—the dark, the cold water, killer dolphins. There can be zero thought of failure or quitting once the fighting starts. Looking back now, I can see that my confidence grew stronger with every experience, in training and in combat. The sense of purpose I had learned from my parents had gotten me started, and once my confidence kicked in, I was on my way to becoming an effective operator and an asset to the team.

Of course, I still had a lot to learn.

CHAPTER 3

The Three-Foot World

Fear

My body was frozen against the smooth rock face.

I couldn't move no matter how much I willed myself to get going. I could feel my arms shaking from the weight. Sweat ran down my face and my palms were damp, making my attempt to hold on even harder. My eyes shifted to the right and caught a glimpse of the glittering Las Vegas Strip far in the distance. I quickly closed my eyes, shaking my head and hoping when I opened them again I'd be in a better place.

When I finally opened my eyes, I was still more than one hundred and fifty feet up, barely hanging on to my hand- and footholds. I had a rope hooked to me, but I had no intention of testing its strength, because that meant falling, which was what I was scared of in the first place.

I had been a SEAL for four years, but I still hadn't mastered my intense fear of heights. The rock face looked like a sheet of brown glass, with no place to get a handhold. My mind and body were in a full-on civil war. My mind screamed at me to move, but my body refused. All I could do was hold on and curse myself for losing one hundred percent of my focus.

By this early point in my career, I'd been on one training deployment to the Pacific and my platoon was training for its next rotation, which would be to Iraq, and which would be my first chance to get into combat. As we got toward the end of the training cycle, one of the last trips was to Red Rock Canyon outside of Las Vegas. I'd gone on one other climbing trip, where I learned the basics, but on this trip we were going to learn how to lead climb and set our own protection.

I've never been a fan of heights, and I sure wasn't thinking about falling or my fear of heights when I signed up for the trip. I was only thinking of downtime in Vegas and blowing off steam before heading to Iraq.

The night we arrived, we hit the Strip and enjoyed all Vegas had to offer. After a few hours of sleep—more like a quick nap—we drove out to the climbing site. We hired civilian instructors and they watched in awe as we pulled new, top-shelf gear out of our rental cars. I had the best gear that money could buy, and the command had hired the best instructors in the world, but I had none of the skills. I was definitely out of my league, especially compared to the professional instructors.

The five instructors were gathered in a group near the parking lot when we arrived. They wore ratty shorts, shirts, and sandals. Climbers are inherently poor, especially the good ones, because climbing is all they do. These guys don't have any other hobbies. I'd seen the same thing with skydivers. All of their money went right back into buying gear and doing the sport that they loved. Our instructors came over to help with the gear, shaking our hands and welcoming us to the canyon. Their hands were callused from hours on the rock face.

The first two days were no big deal. It was more of a refresher, with nothing too high or hard to climb. We had to make sure that everyone remembered the safety precautions and basics we had learned previously before getting into the newer, more demanding climbing the last day.

We split up into two-man teams. Each team had its own instructor. I was paired with Jeff, one of the newer SEALs in the platoon. He wasn't a fan of heights either. There was no way I was going to show my fear, and Jeff was trying hard to hide his nerves from me as well. If your teammates ever see a weakness, you'll never hear the end of it.

Our "billy-goat" instructor led us over to one of the climbing routes. He was short and stocky, with leathery skin and a long goatee. He had the strongest handshake I'd ever felt. A North Face beanie covered his scraggly brown hair. He was an ex-con who'd been to jail for assault. He'd beat up the guy who was banging his wife, or at least that's what he told us during one of the breaks.

It was decided that I'd go first while Jeff would belay as I climbed. I kept up a steady soundtrack of what I was doing as I inched up the cliff face. None of my talking made sense. It was sort of gibberish, but it was comforting for me. I am sure it annoyed Jeff.

"Oh yeah, lucky cam number four," I said, holding the cam in my open hand. "Lucky blue number four."

Each camming device was a different color, based on the size. I set my own "pro," or my own protection, as I climbed. That meant it was up to me to do it right, because if I fell— something I was trying not to think about at the time—the rope would be pulled taut in the camming devices. We were taught to place the cams roughly every ten feet into cracks in the rock face and ledges. If I fell with my closest cam being ten feet below me, I'd fall a total of twenty feet before the rope caught me. If I'd placed that cam wrong, I didn't want to think about falling to the next one below that.

I decided to put them in at five-foot intervals as I climbed, in an attempt to make myself feel more comfortable.

"Yep, every five feet works great," I said to myself as I set another cam into the rock face.

I made it up the first pitch without issue and belayed Jeff as he climbed up. Jeff led the next route, and I stayed below him to belay his climb. Once we both had several chances to practice our lead climbing techniques, the instructor took us up to a bigger wall. The shadow of the wall seemed to stretch out for miles. I tried not to look up to the top of the cliff, which blocked out the sun.

"You're first," the instructor said to me.

I didn't have much to say this time. I was too nervous to talk. This rock face was much bigger and flatter than the others we had climbed. There were half the hand- and footholds available, and we would have to stay very focused on choosing a clean route up the face.

I climbed quickly at first, easily finding hand- and footholds. As I climbed, I set pro into cracks or pockets in the rocks. I had been in such a good rhythm between climbing and setting my pro that I hadn't noticed I was using entirely too many camming devices and was about to run out. Placing my last cam into a big crack in the rock, I was officially stuck. I couldn't go any higher. To be honest, I didn't want to.

For the first time since I started to climb, I took my eyes off the rock face in front of me and started to look around. I was pretty fucking high up. I could see the Las Vegas Strip and the desert stretching all the way to the horizon. I glanced down and saw Jeff, now a lot smaller. He looked like a garden gnome.

Any chance I had of keeping my fear in control was slipping away, a lot like my hold on the rock.

I wished I was anywhere else as I looked up into the crystal-clear blue sky. I was nervous and could feel myself losing focus on where my hand- and footholds should be. I lost "front sight focus." When a SEAL shoots, we talk about focusing on the front sight of our pistol just before we pull the trigger because if it is lined up on the target and in focus, the bullet will hit. If you lose that front sight focus, you'll miss, simple as that.

But all I could think about was the cold rock face, how high I was off the ground, and the instructor climbing up to me without a rope. I could also hear Jeff on the ground yelling up to me.

"You need me to climb up there and save you?" Jeff said in a smartass tone.

I struggled to find a new handhold, but my fingers were tired.

"I'm about to slip and fall," I thought.

To my left, I heard something scrape against the rocks. I'd been so focused on my situation that I'd forgotten all about our instructor. I'd catch him climbing around like Spider-Man as he waited for me to set the next cam. It made me nervous watching him because he didn't use a rope.

The guide finally scampered up to me. Dangling from a harness across his chest were about a half dozen cams. His crazy billy-goat ass had climbed down and collected up all the un-needed cams I had set below so he could pass them off to me and I could keep climbing. And he'd done it all without any rope or pro of his own, free-climbing around me without giving it a second thought. Somehow that fact wasn't comforting.

A cigarette dangled from his lips as he hung there next to me. With one hand on the rock face, the instructor took a drag of his cigarette and exhaled a cloud of blue smoke. It was obvious I was struggling.

"Hey, man," he said in a lazy, raspy voice. "Just stay in your three-foot world."

I was a couple of hundred feet up the rock face and I could barely think, let alone decipher his cryptic advice.

"What the hell are you talking about, bro?"

"Only focus on your three-foot world," he said. "Focus on what you can affect. You keep looking around, and none of that shit can help you right now, can it?"

I shook my head no.

"You're calculating how far you're going to fall," the instructor said. "You're looking down at Jeff, but he's not going to come up and help. You're looking out at the Strip. What are you going to do, gamble your way to the top? Don't look at me. I'm not going to help you either. This is up to you. You're climbing this rock. Stay in your three-foot world."

I'll never forget those words: "Stay in your three-foot world."

It was the only way I got off the rock face. Now reloaded with cams, I focused on wedging one into the nearest crevice. I slid the rope through the carabiner and started to climb again. My focus never went farther than my next hand- or foothold. All the beauty of the desert or Las Vegas sparkling in the distance was lost on me. But I could tell you every crack in the rock. I was so focused it shocked me when my hand reached over the lip of the cliff at the top of the climb.

I finished the climbing trip that week with a new perspective. Staying in my three-foot world became a mantra for me. It is liberating once you let go of the things that you can't control. It seems to work for just about any situation. The three-foot world helped me get through everything from climbing to skydiving to night dives where the only way you can keep your bearings is to focus on the glowing compass on your wrist.

Of course, the other part of being a SEAL that makes a fear of heights a little bit of a problem is skydiving. I had been to jump school even before joining the Navy, but I was uneasy with every jump and it took years before I started to love it.

I remember one jump, just after I graduated S&T. My troop was on a military free-fall training trip in Arizona. I was "new meat," which meant I was the new guy. I had to jump all the gear the more senior guys didn't want to jump, like the collapsible ladder, sledgehammers, and extra ammunition.

The inside of the C-130 was lit by red lights. I couldn't stand up straight as I shuffled onto the plane. It was hot in the cabin as we took off and climbed to twenty thousand feet above the Arizona desert. My mouth was dry and my breathing was ragged. The backpack I was jumping was new, and much bigger than the pack I usually used. It sat at my feet, full of ammunition and extra gear. The straps from the rest of my sixty pounds of gear cut into my skin.

I tried to adjust the weight of the pack, hoping to balance it better, but I didn't have any luck. My body ached from dragging the pack, oxygen tank, and parachutes onto the plane. I rolled my neck, working out the kinks from the heavy helmet and night vision goggles strapped to my head. I just didn't feel comfortable at all. Instead of focusing on what I had to do, I complained to myself about how much everything sucked. All I wanted to do was jump because at least I'd be closer to getting all of the gear off.

Most of the time we wear so much gear that it literally takes all the fun out of something. Jumping at a civilian drop zone wearing a small "sport parachute" can be fun. For our work jumps, I had a minimum of sixty pounds of personal combat gear strapped to me. Add another one hundred pounds from the parachute, an oxygen bottle, and a mask, and then strap an additional sixty-pound backpack of extra "new meat" gear in front of me, and I was weighted down with well over two hundred pounds of gear, doubling my weight.

All my attention was focused on my discomfort when it should have been on the task at hand, a proper exit from the aircraft and the rest of the jump. We were conducting a night jump into an unknown drop zone, meaning we hadn't been there before. I'd studied it on the map—an intersection of two dirt roads near the base of a mountain—but I wouldn't get eyes on it until I was under canopy and looking through my night vision goggles. All I had to do was exit the plane; after a several-second delay, open my chute; and fall into line behind the lead jumper; and, if all went well, we would all land together. We all had the landing zone programmed into the GPS on our wrists in case we weren't able to link up with the lead jumper, but that was usually an unused contingency plan.

It was the lead jumper's job to guide the entire stack to the ground safely. When you are flying collapsible canopies in the middle of the night sky with more than twenty other SEALs, this is easier said than done. Since parachutes aren't rigid like the wing of a hang glider or an airplane, if two parachutes collide with each other, the chutes collapse or wrap around each other, causing you to fall to your death.

I scanned the cabin, looking at my teammates, who were just shadows in the red glow of the lights by the ramp. Most of the guys just sat there silently, occasionally shifting the weight on their laps. It was impossible to see faces or expressions, but no one looked like I felt, which was nervous.

I fiddled with my oxygen tank and repositioned my rifle for the third time. I was so wrapped up in my own suckfest, the whoosh of air as the ramp slowly opened startled me. The jumpmaster gave the signal for "Ramp" and then "Stand up." My teammates, like old men under all the gear, slowly got to their feet and shuffled toward the ramp.

The wind was deafening. We huddled near the edge and waited for the green light to jump. For a second, it dawned on me that I was inside one of the movies that I'd watched growing up. It was surreal, as I looked over my brothers lined up in front of me. I'd worked my ass off to be here.

Had I really made it?

The stars bobbed up and down as the plane settled into its cruising altitude. At this altitude, the black sky was littered so densely with stars it was hard to tell them apart. Beneath us, the clouds slipped by, occasionally breaking open, revealing the black desert below. It was so dark that it was hard to tell the difference between the lights from buildings on the ground and the stars shining in the night sky. I looked at the green numbers on my altimeter.

We got the "One minute" call from the jumpmaster and my mind began to wander. I could feel myself starting to question if I could really handle what was about to come my way. The what-ifs started to circle in my mind.

"What if I screw up my exit?"

"What if I didn't pack my parachute correctly and it doesn't open like it should?"

"What if I can't find the lead jumper and I am lost in the night sky?"

Then the green "go" light lit up.

"Green light. Jumper, go!"

My teammates waddled forward and disappeared off the ramp. Just like in the fifty-meter underwater swim, I needed to force all the what-ifs out of my mind and focus. As my boots reached the lip of the ramp, my mind was still racing. I wasn't focused.

I squared my feet on the ramp with my toes hanging slightly over the edge and pushed off. Nothing about my exit was relaxed or graceful. I was stiff off the ramp and my body position was bad from the start. My head should have been up, and my arms and legs out, controlling my body angle. But as soon as I hit the jet stream flowing off the plane, I started to spin. A spin is the last thing you want exiting an aircraft, especially when you're carrying a lot of weight from extra gear.

The stars were just a smear of light as I rotated like a top. I struggled to get my bearings. A feeling of panic welled up from my chest. I was gulping down air as I flailed in a desperate attempt to stop the spinning. I was in trouble, but I couldn't clear my mind and think, which only compounded my problems.

Instead of worrying about my body position, instead of worrying about getting under control and getting into a stable position, belly to the earth, all I could think was how I had to save myself.

"This is not good; this is not what should be happening right now," went around in my head in a loop.

Out of pure instinct driven by fear, I reached in and pulled the handle to release my main chute. It was too early to pull my chute and I was in an uncontrolled spin; it was the last thing I should have done, but there was no reversing it now. I could feel the chute jump off my back as it came out of the container. In the split second I waited for the jerk of the parachute filling with air, I scolded myself for being so unfocused. I knew everything I did wrong. I fucked up my exit from the aircraft. My body position was stiff and I'd caused the spin to occur. I didn't stop the spin before pulling my chute. I panicked and simply stopped thinking and acting and instead made another mistake by not getting into the proper position before I pulled. I knew better than to make any of those mistakes.

I felt the parachute jerk and the spinning begin to slow, but when I looked up to check my canopy, I couldn't lift my head. The risers that led from my harness up to the parachute blocked it. I could feel the risers pressing against my neck. I thrashed my head back and forth, hoping to wiggle free, but it only put more pressure on the back of my head.

Something was very wrong.

All I could hear was my breathing through my oxygen mask and the flapping of the parachute above me. I took a quick look at my altimeter. I was finally remembering all the basic skydiving rules that I had been taught.

"Always be altitude aware."

I was at eighteen thousand feet, so I had plenty of altitude and time to fix the problem with my chute. But not much time, if I wanted to stay with the others. By now, my teammates were above me, I figured, and with good parachutes they were probably already flying toward the target.

I could hear the snapping of the parachute above me as I started to bank into a lazy turn. At first it was a slow circle, but by the second rotation I was picking up speed. I'd seen the videos of guys with parachutes rolled tight like cigarettes burning into the ground. My parachute had some lift, because I wasn't falling like a meteor. But I had no ability to control my chute, and the spinning was getting faster and faster. I feared if the spinning became too violent I'd lose consciousness.

I had to act.

All of a sudden my mind started focusing on my emergency procedures, snapping me into my three-foot world. Up until this point I was worried about my comfort and how the older guys were going to make fun of me for fucking up my exit. But none of those things were in my three-foot world. Worrying about that wasn't going to help me with my parachute malfunction.

An eerie calm came over me, washing away the panic and discomfort. First I had to find a way to see my malfunctioning parachute.

As I turned, I craned my neck, and I could just make out the parachute. One side was fat and full of air. The other fluttered limply like a bird's broken wing. I'd caused the malfunction when I pulled my parachute handle in the middle of an uncontrolled spin. I was so out of control that the pilot chute, which drags the main chute out of the pack, got tangled on some of the steering lines at the edge of my canopy. The pilot chute was preventing the main chute from opening fully.

There was no way I was going to save this parachute. My only chance was to cut away from the main parachute and pull the reserve. I was picking up more and more speed. The constant revolutions were making me dizzy. It was impossible to focus on the horizon.

We're taught how to deploy our reserve parachutes over and over again until it becomes muscle memory. I took a deep breath, looked down at my cutaway handle, and pulled it. I could feel the main chute break away, and for a split second I started to free-fall again. Once the main chute cleared, a static line pulled the reserve chute. It sprung open and jerked me to a halt.

I immediately looked up to check if I had a good reserve canopy. I hoped like hell that I did, because we don't have another reserve. The main and reserve chute were it. Above me, the reserve parachute was full and fat with air. It flapped gently in the breeze. I pulled on the steering lines to make sure everything was working. Before I keyed the radio to report to the lead jumper, I took a split second to enjoy the silence. It's a crazy silence you can experience only when you're floating through the night sky under a parachute.

I could hear the lead jumper checking in, and I looked at

my GPS and altimeter and got my bearings. They were already headed for the landing zone.

"This is jumper twelve," I said over the radio. "I had a cutaway. I'm at eighteen thousand feet and my distance to target is ten kilometers. I don't have you in sight."

"Roger, jumper twelve," the lead jumper said. "We're at twenty thousand feet. Our distance to target is eight kilometers. My heading is one, four, five degrees."

I pulled on the steering lines, turning in a sweeping arc to get online with the target and the rest of the jumpers. I slowed my descent and stayed on track. Soon, in the distance, I could see my teammates' parachutes. I worked my way back into the stack as we closed in on the landing area. By the time we landed I was right in the middle with the other jumpers.

I grounded my parachute and gathered up my gear. All of the guys around me were jovial, happy with the jump. But I was pissed at myself for making such a rookie mistake. I let fear control me. I wasn't focused and it could have cost me my life.

When it was time to patrol, I got into line and marched to the rendezvous with the buses. I stowed my gear and took a seat near the back, still going over the jump in my head. I was the new guy and couldn't afford to make stupid mistakes. Making it worse, I'd made more than one mistake. I realized my jump was less than perfect from the start. The moment I stepped on the C-130 I was focused on how uncomfortable I was and not on what I was about to do. What if I'd pulled that shit in a firefight? I knew damn well a gunshot wound was going to be a lot more uncomfortable than an ill-fitting pack. I was too worried about all the shit that couldn't directly affect me that night, rather than focusing on all the stuff I could control, and that could kill me.

I needed to know my gear better. From that day, I focused on making sure everything I wore always fit the same and I was always comfortable, or at least as comfortable as two hundred pounds of gear strapped to your body can feel. The obsession went beyond jumping. All of my uniforms and kit fit and were comfortable. I became really good at making sure that if something wasn't fitting right, I was going to take the time to make sure it was near perfect. And it wasn't just the gear I was issued that I obsessed over, but gear I helped design.

But being uncomfortable on the plane was only the first problem. Once my exit went to shit, I started to panic. That is a mistake that more often than not is fatal. Once I stayed in my three-foot world, I got back on track. Instead of looking outward to solve the problem, I focused on the things I could control.

The buses dropped us off at the airport, where we unpacked and met to do an AAR. Everyone on the jump sat down at tables in the briefing room. The lead jumper started going over the mission. Each jumper chimed in with any issues. It finally got to me.

"I had a bad exit," I said. "My main chute malfunctioned. I had to go to my reserve."

After the debrief, one of the team leaders pulled me aside.

"Hey," my team leader said. "So what caused the malfunction?"

"I had a bad exit," I said.

"I know," my team leader said. "Why? What caused the bad exit?"

"I didn't have good body position," I said. "When I started spinning, I got nervous and pulled my main. It's because I was so unstable when I pulled my main that I think I caused the malfunction."

We sat together for the next few minutes going over the jump. I know now that he wanted to make sure I learned from my mistakes.

"Walk through putting your gear on," he said. "Walk through the procedures inside the aircraft, your body position on exit, your emergency procedures. Then last but not least, walk through in your mind what you're going to do while flying your canopy."

The team leader stressed the need to walk through the whole jump in my mind, prior to doing it. It is something I do before every jump now.

People think SEALs are fearless. Think again. No one lives without fear; heights were my Achilles' heel. I probably should have thought of that before leaping at the chance to go to Las Vegas on the Navy's dime. I should have used that fear to master the skydiving procedures from the beginning. I guess I needed a close call to learn a lesson I'll never forget.

Instead of focusing on the fear and being afraid, I have learned to focus on what I can control. I control my gear. I control my rehearsals, and I control my mind and my decision making.

Now, when I hear the drone of the C-130 propellers, I'm excited. I'm the one cracking jokes and looking forward to the views as I silently glide under canopy to the drop zone.

It took me a long time to get that comfortable. To get there, I faced my fear head-on. I volunteered for every jump trip I could at the beginning of my career. I didn't like it, but I knew that if I was going to get any better at it, I was going to have to make myself jump every opportunity I got. The Navy SEALs motto is "The only easy day was yesterday," and throughout my career that was a fact. I always pushed myself and never sat back and rested. I pushed myself every chance I got and tried to make myself better. Each day was always harder than my last.

Slowly I learned to overcome the fear of jumping. I am still not a huge fan of heights, but skydiving doesn't faze me now.

On the ride back to the hotel after the uncontrolled spin, I started to feel better and knew I would handle the same situation better the next time. I couldn't help thinking back to being on the rock face all those years earlier and the simple advice I'd gotten from the human billy goat, back before I'd seen any combat and before I really knew what fear was.

"Hey, man, stay in your three-foot world."

CHAPTER 4
The Hooded Box

Stress

I was in complete darkness.

I could feel the weight of multiple sets of eyes all focused on me. Sweat rolled off my forehead, making the fabric of the hood stick to my face. People were moving around and talking, but I couldn't make out what they were saying. All of my senses—except my eyes—were hypersensitive as I strained to pick up anything that could help me when the hood came off.

I had been on two deployments—including one rotation to Iraq—before I was picked for the S&T course. When it was my turn to enter the box, I slid a magazine full of Simunitions, a paint cartridge created by General Dynamics that can be fired through our rifles, into my weapon and walked to the center of the room. Lights hung from the unfinished ceiling and a catwalk crisscrossed the room, allowing instructors to watch the action from above. The concrete floor was clean. A square box was taped onto the floor at one side of the room. I stood in the middle of the box and the instructors lowered the hood over my head. We couldn't move outside of the taped lines or the exercise would end.

The hood and a rope that was tied to it were attached to a pulley system. When the instructors yanked the rope, the hood came off and I'd have to react to the scenario in front of me. Under the hood, I didn't know if I would have to react to a hostage situation, deal with unarmed but violent bystanders, or handle compliant individuals who could become hostile in a split second. The scenario might be something I'd never encountered before.

Unlike BUD/S, which tested a candidate's will more than anything else, S&T was all about skill, mental control, and the ability to make the right decision under enormous stress and pressure. I had to be able to quickly assess the situation, prioritize the threats, and act accordingly, all with the instructors watching from the catwalk and cataloging every action. Everything was graded to the finest point: One mistake could mean an early exit from the course and a ride back to SEAL Team Five.

I took two deep breaths and closed my eyes as the hood came down to rest on my shoulders. I wiggled my fingers and grabbed the pistol grip of my rifle, my finger lying across the trigger housing. I tried to relax. I knew if I was tense and not thinking clearly I would make a mistake. I didn't think about any what-ifs. I trusted that I would know what to do. The question was whether I would be able to make the right life-or-death decisions quick enough and in the correct order. The S&T course forces you to stretch beyond your three-foot world.

Fear and stress are two different things.

Staying in your three-foot world is one of the keys to

managing fear. But stress is harder to manage because it is usually coming from outside your control. The instructors did their best to throw more stress at us than we could handle.

As the seconds ticked off under the hood, it became harder and harder to stay focused. It felt like the instructors were just fucking with me by making me wait. Maybe they just wanted to see how long I'd stand at the ready. Maybe they were all just standing there laughing at me under the hood. I wiggled my hands again and shifted my weight from foot to foot, trying not to let my mind wander.

I knew it wouldn't take more than a few seconds, a minute at most, but every second under the hood felt like a year.

Then, without warning, the hood was gone.

The light hit me like a flashbulb. I immediately started to scan the room with my rifle up and at the ready. Not ten feet in front of me stood a cute blond woman. I could see her soft brown eyes looking at me. She was wearing jeans and a T-shirt. She smiled at me like she knew something I didn't.

Not seeing a weapon in her hands, I scanned past her. I caught a glimpse of a gunman, dressed in a team ball cap, T-shirt, and cargo pants, over the girl's shoulder. He was in the back right corner of the room holding a black semiautomatic pistol to a man's head. The hostage had his head down, and I couldn't see his face.

Not even thinking about it, I'd already shouldered my gun and my eyes were already looking through my sights. He didn't say anything as I set the red dot of my EOTech sight on his head.

"Hey, buddy," I heard over my shoulder. "Hey, asshole!"

"Holy shit," I thought. I hadn't even looked behind me. "Fuck, I'm already spiraling out of control." I hadn't even taken a look at the entire room. I was too focused on the two threats in front of me.

I flipped my safety off and fired off two quick shots. The paint rounds exploded on the gunman's chest. I knew I needed to take care of the immediate threat with the hostage first. Even if there were armed people behind me, in my mind at that moment, the hostage situation was the first priority. I watched the gunman drop his pistol and drop to the ground next to the hostage in a piss-poor attempt to play dead.

Even though the gunman was now dead, I felt as if I'd already screwed up. I hadn't even assessed the entire room. I was in too much of a rush. Early on in my career, I had a hard time slowing things down because we were trained to do everything at full speed.

During my first deployment to Iraq with SEAL Team Five, we ran to the door and up the stairs with lots of yelling and screaming during every raid. Hell, when we arrived in Iraq, nobody in my platoon had any combat experience. It was the first deployment for most of the platoon. We were basically making it up as we went along.

We set up our camp behind a palace that sat on a massive man-made hill on the outskirts of Baghdad International Airport. From the roof of the palace, I could see the airport spread out in front of me. Military aircraft—big gray C-130s and C-17s—lumbered down the runways. There seemed to be a constant hum of engines and the thump of helicopter rotors. Baghdad International Airport was a massive hub for Coalition forces. HUMVEES and LMTV trucks kicked up dust on the dirt roads that led from the airfield to the tent cities where the troops lived. Contractors raced around in four-by-four trucks, and every day a new field of modular trailers sprang up to be used for sleeping or to serve as offices for the various companies.

A Special Forces team occupied the main palace. A massive wooden door opened into a foyer with marble floors. Stairs led up to the second-floor rooms. There was a chow hall built on the back, and the operations center took over one of the downstairs rooms. As I walked around the palace, I could see the design work on the marble and the fine craftsmanship on the banister. But looters had stolen most of the valuables before we arrived. Massive holes in the walls were everywhere. The rumor during the invasion was Saddam's palaces had gold pipes, so looters all over Iraq punched holes in the walls looking to make a little cash.

Outside sat big olive-green antennas and a satellite dish. Generators hummed near the pool, which separated the main palace and our living quarters. We took the servants' houses near the motor pool. Like the palace, the quarters had marble floors. But the floors lacked the ornate patterns, and there were fewer signs of wealth. That didn't stop the looters from punching holes in the walls out there too.

The pool area became the camp's center. Both SEALs and Special Forces lounged by the water between missions. It was early spring, and the oppressive heat hadn't arrived. But during the afternoons, the temperature hit the high eighties. We mostly worked nights, so there was little to do but eat, sleep, work out, and sit by the pool until we got a mission.

Within weeks of arriving, we had morphed into a Baghdad SWAT team, raiding compounds of suspected insurgents with the help of the CIA. The agency was trying to round up insurgent leaders, who were mostly former Baath party members. The CIA would get a tip, and that night we'd hit the house.

About midway through the deployment, we got called in to detain a former Iraqi Air Force intelligence officer. We all met in the operations center. Our CIA contact, dressed in a dark polo shirt, khaki pants, and desert boots, walked us through the intelligence. The target was organizing attacks against American soldiers in the city. A CIA informant tipped off the Coalition and the information worked its way through the system to us. The Iraqi officer was tall and skinny, with no facial hair, rare in Iraq.

The informant would drive ahead of our convoy and mark the house. We'd follow behind him, crash through the gate, and storm the house. There wasn't a lot of finesse in the way we did it, just a lot of yelling and explosions.

We met around eleven at night to do a final mission brief and left the wire just after midnight. The CIA officer and his informant were well ahead of us in a beat-up old sedan with mismatched panels. We rode in three HUMVEES with mounted machine guns. I'd worked with a teammate to weld running boards and some handholds on the roof so guys could hang off the sides and launch more quickly once we got to the target, similar to what you'd see a SWAT team using in downtown LA.

I rode in the lead vehicle. The streets were deserted. The streets were narrow with a tangle of wires crisscrossing above. The truck's antennas whipped back as they hit the wires above, and the throaty rumble of the engine made it hard to hear anything. Bursts of radio traffic cut through the engine noise.

"OK, that's it," I heard the officer in charge of the mission say. "Chemlights on the left."

The engine of the HUMVEE revved and the truck surged forward, coming to a halt in front of the compound. I was practically out of the truck before it stopped. The main gate was ajar and I ran through the short courtyard to the front door. I didn't try the doorknob to see if it was locked. My teammate stuck a breaching charge across the lock, and we both rolled to the side of the door.

"Fire in the hole," my teammate yelled. A few seconds later, he set off the charge, blowing the door off its hinges and sending it flying inside the house. I didn't wait for the smoke to clear. I was inside seconds after the door, my gun up and ready to fire.

I could hear my teammates clamoring behind me. We were like sharks in a feeding frenzy. I could feel the adrenaline, making it hard for me to focus. The spring heat, even at midnight, was still muggy, and I could feel the sweat pooling in my gloves as I scanned for a target.

The house was nice, with smooth marble floors and stairs. Oriental rugs covered the floors of the downstairs rooms, and the smell of cooking oil hung in the air. The foyer opened up into two rooms on either side of the hall. The kitchen was toward the back of the house, to the right of a staircase that led to the second floor.

Behind me, I heard my teammates clearing into the first-floor rooms. I kept moving forward toward the staircase.

"Get the fuck down," a teammate said.

"We got 'im," said another teammate. "Get his hands."

The Iraqi Air Force officer was in the downstairs living room. He gave up immediately, and my teammates quickly bound his hands. I watched them shove him out the door to the waiting trucks. I could hear a woman and at least one child sobbing in the living room, as the rest of the team spread out.

Our platoon chief stood in the center of the hallway as the "hall boss" and yelled out directions to different rooms as we cleared.

"Clear left!"

"Clear right!"

"Moving!"

I moved to the bottom of the stairs with a teammate and held security on the stairs.

As I approached the bottom of the stairs, the foyer exploded in a barrage of AK-47 rounds. The bullets crashed into the marble floor, sending shards into the air. I could hear my teammates yelling and diving for cover as the rounds smashed into the walls just feet in front of me.

I quickly backed away from the stairs. I could feel the marble showering me as I ducked away from the burst. The roar of the AK-47 echoed through the first floor of the house, and thick smoke and the smell of gunpowder hung in the air, making it impossible to hear or think. Someone was spraying rounds down the stairs. The gunman wasn't aiming as much as pointing the barrel in our direction and holding down the trigger. None of the fire was accurate, but that didn't matter with the shooter only fifteen feet away from us.

I wheeled around and started to fire up the stairs with my M-4, hoping to force the shooter to find cover.

At least three of us were now returning fire when our platoon chief came up and started to organize us for an assault up the steps. The gunman had the advantage. We couldn't see where he was hiding above us. We had no idea if it was just one or multiple shooters. Close air support from a fast mover or AC-130 was what we needed, but we were in downtown Baghdad. The threat of causing civilian casualties was too great. Our only choice was to assault up the stairs and clear the second floor.

The thick smoke was making it harder and harder to see.

The chief called for flash-crash grenades. The grenades are nonlethal and just make a ton of noise, stunning the target for a few seconds. The grenades would hopefully stun the gunman long enough for us to make our assault up the stairs.

We had about a half dozen grenades. They look like small silver pipes with holes in the body. We pulled the pins and tossed them up to the second floor. The booms and crashes sounded like the end of the world. My ears were ringing and I had to yell to communicate with the guy next to me.

My teammate and I took a quick glance at each other as the noise of the flash-crash started to taper off. We both knew it was time to head up the stairs. I took two deep breaths and tried to relax and stay focused on exactly what I needed to do.

The grenades smashed the second-floor windows, and shards of glass littered the marble steps and floor. A heavy, acidic, white smoke hung in the hall. We both fired into the thick smoke at the top of the stairs as we climbed. It was a feeble attempt at providing some covering fire.

I got about four shots off and was halfway up the stairs when my M-4 jammed. There was no time to fix it, so I let it drop. My rifle hung across my chest as I slid my pistol out of the holster on my leg.

Sweat ran down my face, into my eyes. I tried hard to focus on my front sight as I picked my way down the hall, trying to avoid stepping on the glass. I knew at any second the gunman might jump out and start firing again. There was no cover in the hallway. If he showed his face, he was getting shot.

There were three rooms on the second floor of the house. A balcony was at the far end of the hall. My teammates were right behind me. The SEAL beside me cleared into the first room on the right with some of the other guys. It was littered with sleeping mats. I continued slowly making my way down the hallway through the thick smoke.

As we approached the second door on the right side of the

hallway, I stepped past it as my teammates behind me entered the room. As we got to the last door along the hallway on the left, my teammates smashed it open and flooded inside. I could hear yelling from the guys in the second room on the right side of the hallway. They found an AK-47, but there was no sign of the gunman.

Directly in front of me at the end of the hallway was the door to the balcony. I reached out and tried the handle. It was locked. My teammates had found an AK-47, but no one knew where the gunman had gone. I had an idea.

I thought through the risks. Did he have a suicide vest on? Was there more than one shooter? There was still no sign of him inside. I was starting to get nervous. How had the motherfucker gotten away already?

He couldn't go down the steps. I took a knee and quickly unjammed my M-4. I unlocked the balcony door and slowly opened it up. Maybe he was hiding outside. It hadn't dawned on me that there was no way he could have escaped outside and locked the door from the inside. It had all happened so quickly, and there was so much stuff going on around me it was hard to focus on the little things, like the balcony door being locked from the inside. I was obviously a bit overwhelmed. The whole fight was like being in a car accident.

When you're in a car accident, you probably remember the last two to three seconds leading up to the crash. If you were in another car accident, and then another and another, you would begin to remember more and more details about what happened to cause each crash, as you got more familiar with the sights, smells, sounds, rhythms, and speed of a crash.

Gunfights are like car crashes to some degree. They are things you try to avoid, they always surprise you when they happen, and because of the rush of adrenaline, it can become hard to focus and make good decisions. This was one of my first firefights, and I was having trouble staying focused.

With my M-4 jam cleared and the rifle back in action, I opened the door and cleared out onto the balcony.

No one was there. Where the fuck had he gone? I walked down to the end of the balcony, searching the courtyard below and the roof above. I could see our idling trucks in front of the house. There was no way he could have jumped down and escaped. The gunman had vanished.

At the end of the balcony I peered into the window of the room where they'd found the AK-47. I could see my teammates standing in the room. It looked like they'd searched under the beds and in the wooden armoire at the far end of the room.

I was about to walk back into the house when I spotted an adult male through the window, inside the room with my teammates. He was tucked in the windowsill, hidden by a piece of furniture. The male was in his early twenties, wearing a wife-beater T-shirt and shorts. His hair was a mess and he had a few wisps of a beard on his cheeks. His knees were pressed into his chest and I could tell he was trying to be as still as possible. He had his eyes closed and he had no idea I could see him.

I leveled my M-4, but I couldn't shoot. He was unarmed, and besides, my teammates were standing behind him and a stray bullet could hit them. Thick black metal bars covered the window. I slid the barrel of my rifle between the bars and smashed the glass. The breaking glass startled the gunman and he turned to face me.

I reared back and drove the muzzle of my rifle into his face. His head snapped back and his lip split open, sending blood cascading down his chin and onto his dirty wife-beater T-shirt. He groaned and fell out of the windowsill onto the bedroom floor. Some of my teammates grabbed him, flipped him over on his face, and cuffed him with a plastic zip tie. We found out afterward he was the Iraqi officer's son. He'd ditched his AK-47 before hiding in the windowsill.

It was impossible for me to focus once we got back to base that night. I kept going over the mission in my head. The guys who found the AK-47 should have found the son, but none of us managed the stress of the situation very well.

It wasn't until a couple years later, and the hooded box test, that I started to really think about how to manage stress. I learned there that the key was to first prioritize all the individual stressors and then act. I break it all down into the little things I can manage. The stressors that I can't affect, I don't worry about. The ones I can affect, I simply deal with one at a time. In a lot of ways, it goes back to BUD/S and the elephant.

You know, how do you eat an elephant? One bite at a time.

The hooded box test is meant to overwhelm. It is meant to force you to make very difficult decisions, right or wrong, good or bad, life or death, all in seconds. We face the same challenge in combat. I always tried to keep things as simple as possible. We don't want guys to freeze when faced with multiple threats. But we also don't want guys to immediately start shooting without assessing the situation. Take what's there, assess the situation, prioritize, and break it down into small tasks you know you can accomplish or eliminate or fix immediately. Through constant practice, repetition, and experience, most SEALs can prioritize stressors fast enough that it feels more like an instinct than a process.

Once that happens, everything starts slowing down.

Take the hooded box drill from S&T. I shot the hostage taker with two paint rounds seconds after the instructors pulled off the hood. He was the first box on my checklist. The second box was the men behind me. I swung around and yelled at the two men behind me.

"Show me your hands," I barked, keeping my rifle up and at the ready. "Get the fuck back!"

The men were dressed like the gunman in cargo pants and team shirts. But the men were unarmed and held up their hands right away. Both men slowly backed up, taking very small, deliberate steps. Once they were a few feet away, I told them to get down on the ground.

"Put your face on the floor," I said. "Spread your arms out."

They did what I ordered, and I turned to face the blonde again, but she had a pistol out and stuck it in my face.

"What the fuck are you doing?" an instructor yelled from the catwalk above me.

The instructors all started yelling at me for not acting quickly enough. I was too deliberate. I didn't move from threat to threat quickly enough and it cost me. Luckily, just about everyone failed the first time. Car crash number one complete, and it wasn't pretty.

I cursed myself for being so slow. I spent too much time on the men and forgot about the woman. I didn't see her as a threat, but overseas plenty of women, in Iraq specifically, would hide cell phones and weapons. On my first deployment with SEAL Team Five, we searched a woman after we arrested her husband, and found several phones and guns. During that same deployment, four women were arrested in Baghdad wearing suicide-bombing belts. A few months after the Baghdad arrests, a female suicide bomber—dressed like a man—detonated a suicide bomb outside of Tall Afar in northern Iraq. The insurgents knew we didn't search women. After that, we made a point of searching everyone on target.

I'd failed my first hooded box test at S&T, but the lesson learned wasn't one I'd forget. Assess, prioritize, and act. I'd get in that "car crash" of combat hundreds of more times throughout my career, facing new stresses faster than I could have imagined back during the hooded box training, firing real rounds instead of nonlethal paint, my life and the lives of others on the line. I learned something vital every single time.

CHAPTER 5

Safe Return Doubtful

Mind-set

I slid my rifle behind me and started to climb up the metal ladder. I could hear it scrape against the side of the building as I reached for the next rung.

Ahead of me, my teammate had already reached the roof and slid over the small parapet wall. I reached the roof seconds later and climbed over, dragging more than sixty pounds of body armor and gear with me. Below, I could see my teammates slowly moving into position at the front door of the target.

We were the "roof team," which meant we provided overwatch from the high ground. We were about to hit an insurgent safe house, and it was my team's job to get to the roof to cover the assault. If we were able to enter the building from the roof, we assaulted down the stairs while the ground element assaulted up the stairs. Theoretically, we would capture the bad guys in the middle and hopefully before they had time to resist.

It was 2006 and Iraq was the big priority. The Army unit assigned had taken some heavy casualties and needed replacements. I was only about a month into my first deployment with my own unit when my six-man team was sent from Afghanistan over to Iraq to help. At first, we thought our entire team would be attached as a unit, but when we arrived we got separated and sent individually to different teams.

We flew into the military side of Baghdad International Airport and drove to the Green Zone, a walled-off area of the Iraqi capital occupied by Coalition forces. I'd been to Iraq with SEAL Team Five, so everything looked familiar. Toward the end of that deployment, I'd operated in Baghdad. At that time, we were all new, with little to no combat experience. But landing in Baghdad this time, it felt different. There was energy in the air, a confidence that pervaded the entire military because of our collective combat experience.

I was still pretty new to my team, and I'd never worked with the Army but had heard rumblings about how the two services did not get along. There was always this competition between the two, probably driven by our shared quest to be the best. There were shooting competitions and other drills that always seemed to pit the two units against each other. In my mind, I expected to see or experience this tension, but it never came. All the old-school drama over which unit was better had faded since the war started. We were one team. The team opened up, pulled me in, and made me one of their own. No one cared about which unit shot better when we were all working together fighting a common enemy.

When I landed, Jon, my new team leader, met me at the operations center and took me to my room. He also showed me the chow hall and gym and introduced me to my other teammates. My new team seemed to be made up of guys very much like the SEALs on my old team. We used all the same gear, tactics, and command structure. They were Army, and I was Navy, and there were some cultural differences, but the basic makeup of the guys was very familiar.

Jon welcomed me and included me in all the planning. There was never a moment when I didn't feel like I was part of the team, but more importantly I felt like Jon and the others were open to hearing my opinion.

Once, we were planning a mission a few weeks after I arrived. My team was slated to land on the roof of the target on an MH-6 Little Bird and clear down from the roof. Jon was working on the manifest, the list of guys going on the mission.

"Space is tight on this one, boys," Jon said.

He was crunching the numbers to make sure we stayed under the weight limit. I was sure I'd be cut from the mission. I was the new guy and the SEAL. The planning was over and the rest of my team left the operations center. I got my notebook and headed back to the room.

"Hey," Jon said as I started to leave. "You're on tonight."

Later, I saw Jon talking to the other new guy on the team. He was staying behind. The next time we exceeded the weight limit, I stayed behind. Jon always made it a point to swap me out with his other new guy, ensuring I got as much love as the rest of his team. Yes, I was still considered a new guy both at my unit and the Army team, but it was nice to know that Jon thought of me as part of his team.

After the first few missions, I folded myself into the team, and soon I was no longer looked at as the token SEAL replacement. I was just a teammate, one of two new guys on the team.

I'd just met these guys, but I already trusted them with my life and they did the same. I knew that they would risk their lives to save mine and I'd do the same for them. I credit Jon with making the transition seamless. He was one of the best leaders I've ever worked for in the military. He didn't have the respect of his team and others just because he was the boss. He earned everyone's respect because of his character, his leadership, and his calm demeanor in combat. It seemed like nothing fazed him. I immediately looked up to him as someone I wanted to emulate.

I realized over the course of my career that every special operations unit shared a common mind-set. We were all wired the same way. We all started with a shared sense of purpose. In the past, and in peacetime, there was a rivalry between the units. But once the shooting started, that rivalry was discarded in favor of teamwork, because if there was one thing we all agreed on, it was completing our mission and coming home safe.

If you think of a special operations team—SEALs, Special Forces, Rangers, and the Air Force Pararescuemen and combat controllers—like a boat, everybody rows. The officers down to the newest guy are trained to care about the team first and do what it takes to accomplish the mission. I saw the same mentality when I worked with the international special operations units.

Every single unit I've ever worked or trained with had that in common. Some of the gear and tactics might be a bit different. Some of the units had better toys, but in the end it didn't matter if you had the most expensive rifle or had special training. We all volunteered for the hardest training we could find in our respective countries. We all learned to push ourselves to go well beyond our mental and physical limits.

Units like SEALs and other special operations units have been in existence since war was created. The Greeks had special units and George Washington's army used sharpshooters during the American Revolution.

But only after World War II did officials start figuring out how best to screen and train special operations forces. And the first step was always finding guys with the right mind-set to achieve the group's common goal. Mind-set is the common denominator.

Charlie Beckwith, after arriving in Vietnam in 1965, was given command of Project Delta—Detachment B-52. The reconnaissance unit was created to collect intelligence along the Ho Chi Minh Trail and in South Vietnam. Beckwith fired most of the soldiers in the unit when he took command and started to recruit replacements using a flyer.

> WANTED: Volunteers for project Delta. Will guarantee you a medal, a body bag, or both. Requirements: have to be a volunteer. Had to be in country for at least six months. Had to have a CIB (Combat Infantry Badge). Had to be at least

the rank of Sergeant—otherwise don't even come and talk to me.

He wanted to find guys like my teammates, who possessed a never-quit attitude and a single-minded drive to accomplish the mission. Starting with the mentality from the flyer, Beckwith later created ███████ based on what he learned from the British SAS.

But the military is not the only example. Ernest Shackleton, who led three British expeditions to the Antarctic in the 1900s, reportedly placed an ad in a London newspaper looking for the same type of man:

> Men wanted for hazardous journey. Low wages, bitter cold, long hours of complete darkness. Safe return doubtful. Honor and recognition in event of success.

I would have signed up for Beckwith's Project Delta and Shackleton's expedition.

I never wanted to do anything normal. I can't be average. No one involved in special operations can be average because our missions are never easy or routine. Both Shackleton and Beckwith were looking for a shared sense of purpose and a common mind-set among all their people. If anybody on their crews wasn't there for the right reasons and for the team's needs, there was a higher chance of failure. And failure in the special operations community is never tolerated.

Most nights in Iraq, I was perched on the landing skid of a Little Bird—an MH-6 helicopter flown by the 160th Special Operations Aviation Regiment—racing over the rooftops. I'd fast rope to the roof of a building and clear the top floors while my teammates in the trucks on the street cleared the lower levels. The missions were exactly what I signed up to do, but I was doing them with the Army instead of my SEAL teammates. We were waging a massive campaign to dismantle al Qaeda in Iraq.

We called it "Baghdad SWAT."

But some nights, we didn't have the Little Birds. If we were going to the roof, we had to climb.

As I crested the parapet wall, I looked back over my shoulder and saw that Jon had reached the roof. I turned and headed for the opposite corner, scanning for any targets. Tile covered the roof and a small two-foot-high parapet wall ran completely around the edge. A door sat in the middle of the roof and a myriad of satellite dishes of all makes and models were attached to the corners of the building. Bundles of thick black power lines ran from building to building, sagging over the road and alleyway.

I had a map of the area in my head and knew the target we were looking for was on the other side of the roof. Over the radio, I heard the ground team searching for the correct door. The enemy safe house was in a duplex, but from the radio traffic the ground team was unsure which door to breach and enter.

From my perch three stories up, I could see the ground

team's trucks. I heard a muffled boom, and the Army operators on the ground started to move into the house. I kept watch on the house, waiting for any sign of movement.

Then word came over the radio. The boys hit the wrong side of the duplex. They were going into the other side of the duplex now. I heard a burst from an AK-47 and some yelling.

"We've got squirters," I heard over the radio.

From our vantage point, I knew that the squirters had to be close, but they were out of sight. We couldn't see into the alley located to the north of our location because of the building in front of us. We needed to cross over to the other building, but there was no time to go all the way down to the ground floor, move over to the next building, and then clear our way back up three floors to the roof of the other building.

Nearby on the roof, I noticed a ladder. It looked long enough to reach the parapet wall on the other building. From that roof, we'd have a perfect angle down on the alley the enemy fighters were using to escape.

I looked at Jon, but he was working the radio, which was jammed with reports of fighters on the run. The guys inside the building also found a cache of weapons and explosives.

I wanted to get into the action, so I ran over to the ladder. It was made of discarded pieces of wood nailed together. A single nail and some wire held some of the ladder's rungs on. I grabbed the ladder and put it on my shoulder and ran over to the edge of the building where my teammate waited.

"Think this haji ladder will hold us?" my teammate asked.

We were three stories up. I stood on the lip of the parapet wall and looked across the open space between the buildings. It was about fifteen feet across.

"If we lay it flat and crawl across, I think it will," I said, hoping more than believing it.

"Either way, we're about to find out," he said with a smirk.

We both wanted to get in the fight and stop the squirters from escaping, or worse, setting up an ambush. We gently slid the ladder across the alley. My teammate went first. Lying flat, he slid across the ladder while I held it and kept watch on the other building. When it was my turn, I slung my rifle around behind me so it rested on my back and started to crawl across.

My mind went back to thin ice in Alaska. The only way to get across thin ice is to spread your body weight out as wide as possible. If you stand up, all your body weight is in one spot, and the next thing you know you fall through into freezing-cold water. Like crossing thin ice, crawling across the ladder was very dangerous. We were three stories off the ground, enemy fighters were running around, and we were about to trust this piece-of-shit Iraqi ladder to keep us from falling.

At least in Alaska I hadn't been wearing the additional sixty pounds of gear.

I took two deep breaths and tried to stay focused. This was one of the many times staying in my three-foot world kept me going, because I still hated heights.

Inch by inch I crawled across the alley. Below, I saw a massive pile of trash. Most of it looked like kitchen waste, with rotting food and various food containers. Plastic bags were blown around the alley, and it looked like a car or truck had hit the waste pile, scattering trash into the middle of the alley.

I never stopped moving and finally made it to the other building. Back on my feet, I raced over to the corner, looking for the squirters. The enemy fighters would have easily gotten away had we hesitated or decided not to use the ladder. I picked up the squirters running at a dead sprint just as we got to the edge of the building and looked into the alley. Both men were carrying rifles.

I could see my teammate's laser stop on the fighter on the left. I zeroed in on the fighter on the right. We both opened fire and cut the fighters down before they could get to the mouth of the alley. They had gotten lucky when the ground force hit the wrong side of the duplex, but that's where their luck ran out.

On the other building, Jon heard the shots. Out of the corner of my eye, I could see him hustling over to where we'd left the ladder. I turned back to the alley and kept scanning. My teammates in the house were still clearing rooms and finding weapons, but it was unclear how many fighters were in the safe house.

Above me, I heard AH-6 Little Birds crisscrossing in the sky. They were armed with rockets and machine guns, ready to engage if we ran into trouble. After the first reports of squirters, they started flying in ever-widening circles from the target, looking for fighters who might have escaped.

Then I heard an urgent call over the radio.

"We've got a man down," the Little Bird pilot said.

A few seconds later, the pilot repeated the call.

"We've got a man down."

At first I assumed that the ground force had taken a casualty as they finished clearing the target building. Then the pilot came back with a second report.

"We've got a man down roughly one hundred meters south of the target compound," the pilot said.

That didn't make sense. I was located one hundred meters from the target with Jon and my team. We'd made contact, but the pilot couldn't be talking about us. We were fine. The fighters never got off a round.

I glanced over at my teammate. He shrugged. I turned back to see if Jon was on our roof so I could ask him about the radio call.

Jon was gone.

"Where did Jon go?" I asked my teammate. "He was just there talking on the radio."

"Where's the ladder?" my teammate said.

Shit.

We both sprinted over to the edge of the building. The ladder was gone. I looked over the side and saw Jon lying in the pile of garbage. His helmet was turned to one side and I could just hear a faint moan as he rocked in pain.

"Roger, I've got a visual," I said over the radio. "He is in the alley between the buildings located just south of the target."

The helicopter saw him go down and must have called it in to the guys on the ground. Now the medics wanted to know how to get to him.

"Get on the GRG and let's talk some people in to get him," my teammate said. "We need to get down there now."

We were still getting reports of additional fighters in the area. If they stumbled upon Jon, he was dead. I pulled out my GRG—a gridded reference graphic, which is a small map with the buildings in the area identified by number—and started to guide the guys on the ground to Jon.

GRGs are usually made of satellite photos of the area, and they are often used to call in air strikes by providing the pilots and the guys on the ground with the same point of view.

"Stand by," I said into the radio. "He is down in the alley at the intersection of Echo Four and Delta Eight."

The ground force immediately sent their medical team to the location using the coordinates off the GRG. We stood on the roof and covered him until our teammates entered the alley. Then we started to look for a way off the roof. We couldn't go back to the original building because the ladder was lying in the alley in two pieces. The roof of the new building was identical to the roof of the first, with a door leading downstairs. It was unlocked.

I tried to focus and calm myself down. I was really worried about Jon. Over the months that I'd worked with Jon, he'd become a mentor and a friend. I felt like he and my other teammates were brothers, much like my fellow SEALs. I would hate for anything to happen to him. From my perch on the roof he didn't look so good, but I could hear him moaning and with my medical training I knew that this was at least a good sign.

"Let's go," I heard my teammate whisper as he motioned toward the door that led down into the building.

I slowly moved down the staircase with my rifle raised and ready to fire. It was always a little shocking to enter buildings in Baghdad. From the outside, it was hard to tell what they looked like inside. Many times, we hit houses that looked run-down, only to find nice furniture and fixtures in the rooms.

I had no idea we were on a house when I shimmied across the ladder a few minutes earlier. The stairwell opened into a hallway on the third floor of someone's home. My boots squeaked on the marble floor as we started toward a staircase at the end of the hall. I took a cursory glance in each room as we passed. I wanted to make sure no fighters were there, but that was it. We weren't really clearing the entire house. We needed to make our way to the exit and to Jon.

We came down the marble stairs leading from the third floor to the second floor. The staircase kept going down to the bottom floor. We were on our way down to the second floor when I saw a man standing on the landing just below. He was dressed in a dishdasha, the long robe worn by Arab men, and sandals. His arms were out and half raised like he was making sure I saw he wasn't armed.

"Can I help you?" he said in English and with only a slight accent.

I was about to start yelling at him to get down on the ground, but the near-perfect English startled me.

"We need to get downstairs," I said.

"Follow me," he said.

I got close to him and kept my rifle trained on his back as he led us down to the second floor. I didn't trust him, but I also thought it was unlikely he had fighters in the house. I got the sense he just wanted to make sure we didn't smash up his house trying to find a way out.

"I'm a professor," he said.

I didn't answer. I didn't really care. I just wanted to get out of the house and get to Jon's location. My mission started as a hit, but as soon as Jon got injured, the mission changed.

The professor led us down to the front door and undid the locks. He opened the door and stepped out of our way. My teammate told the professor to move away from the door and stay quiet. I stopped at the threshold and peered out, looking for any fighters. Confident we were safe, I led the way out of the door and into the alley.

In the alleyway, I could see a medic kneeling next to Jon. He was wide-awake and still moaning. He'd fallen three stories down into the alley and landed in the pile of trash. It was likely the only time a pile of Iraqi garbage saved anyone. Most of the time I worried about bombs planted in the piles that lined the streets and alleys of the Iraqi capital.

When we got there, the medic was talking to Jon.

"Can you stand up?" the medic asked him.

"Yeah," he said.

Jon didn't have any broken bones. He let out a long groan as we helped him up and walked him over to the waiting trucks. He slumped down into the back of the truck and let out a deep breath. He was hurting but didn't want to show it.

"Dammit. That sucked. The fucking ladder broke," Jon said.

Jon didn't see us set up the Iraqi ladder, and in the moment, hustling to get to our position after he heard us fire shots, he thought it was one of our metal ladders that we carried on every target. All he had on his mind was getting to us to support in any way that he could.

He decided to walk across instead of crawling over the rungs on his stomach and spreading out the weight like we had done. He tried to walk rung by rung across the ladder, which had been lashed together with old wire and rusty nails. He was three stories in the air, wearing more than sixty pounds of gear, and looking through night vision goggles. Even our goggles, which were some of the best, made depth perception difficult.

The feat would have been hard during the day, and even on a metal ladder, but Jon attempted to do it at night, in combat. He made it halfway and probably would have cleared the entire distance without falling had the ladder not snapped in the center under his weight.

I was stunned listening to him tell us what happened. It took balls to walk across a ladder, at night, during a firefight. I started to kid him that the ladder broke from the weight of his testicles.

We wrapped up the raid soon after and drove back to the

palace. Jon moaned each time the truck hit a rut in the road, and in Iraq all of the roads have ruts. When we got back, he didn't go to the hospital. He sat through the AAR before going to bed. Jon took two days off and then returned to full duty. He'd suffered some bruises, but no serious injuries.

I was relieved to see him two days later on the skid of a Little Bird flying to a new target, but not as relieved as he was. There was no doubt missing a mission and knowing we were going into harm's way without him was worse than any pain from his fall.

I still keep in touch with Jon to this day. In fact, I went to his retirement party last year. It was an intimate affair with only those close to him. Jon still had the thick chest, but no beard. Like me, he looked older. Not from the years, but from the mileage. He gave more than twenty years of service to his country.

Jon calls me his "favorite SEAL." It is a distinction I take great pride in, since not only was he one of the best leaders that I ever worked for in my entire time in the SEALs, but he has also become a lifelong friend. Even after I returned from that deployment in Iraq, and despite our busy schedules, we managed to keep in touch. The conversations were more than just catching up on current events; we'd always compare the latest tactics and techniques used by our respective units. The competition between Army and Navy had officially ended in our minds, and we were one big team that always had each other's backs. Jon was my swim buddy on the "green" side.

I'd arrived in Baghdad a nervous new guy who wasn't sure

I'd click with the Army guys. But I'd learned almost from day one that we had the same mind-set. We shared a common purpose, and that allowed me to become a member of the team. We didn't get caught up in meaningless rivalry based on the color of our uniform. We may use different equipment and have our own selection courses, but we are all the same in our minds.

We all volunteered to go on the most dangerous missions, where, as Beckwith put it, "a medal, a body bag, or both" are common. We can all accept "low wages, bitter cold, long hours of complete darkness" like Shackleton promised, because we'd all rather die than fail.

But most of all, we always put the team over the individual and never accept anything but the best from everyone. Those words are easy to say and write, but hard to live by. But those are the kinds of men I served with in the special operations community, men who share a common sense of purpose and a nearly identical mind-set.

CHAPTER 6
The Setup

Trust

I stood in the operations center staring at a massive flat-screen TV. Next to me, Scott scratched at his beard and shook his head.

"Something isn't right with this," he said.

Scott was one of the older guys on the team. He'd been around enough to know what "right" looked like.

It had been roughly nine years since those first days of training and my first combat deployment in Iraq. The war had moved to Afghanistan and then back to Iraq and finally back to Afghanistan. I'd been on hundreds of missions and hit all kinds of targets. I'd been doing this long enough to know a good target, and nothing about this target made sense.

The compound on the monitor showing the drone's feed looked like every other biscuit-colored house in Afghanistan. The walls—made of rocks and mud—were ten to twelve feet high, with a metal gate. The compound sat in the middle of an open field with farmland all around it. A line of trees bordered the field on one side. Several smaller compounds sat less than half a kilometer away.

No children played in the field. We didn't see any women outside working in the courtyard. No one came in or out of the house. There were no goats or cows around grazing. No men in the nearby fields. The house looked deserted, except that we knew it might contain a high-level al Qaeda commander.

At this point in the war, it was rare to find an al Qaeda commander in Afghanistan. We were mostly tracking and killing little "T" Taliban fighters, who moonlighted between farming and getting their jihad on. The big "T" Taliban leaders were based across the border in Pakistan, where they stayed just out of reach. A legitimate bad guy was smart enough to know better. If an al Qaeda commander was hiding in the house, where was his personal security? No one came to the house to get orders or visit him. Why would an al Qaeda commander come across the border with no security and hang out in a deserted house?

It didn't add up. Scott was dead-on. This target had to be a trap.

It was a conclusion any of us could draw from our shared experience. For the last several years, special operations forces had been hunting Taliban and al Qaeda commanders and bomb makers. We'd determined their pattern of movement and waited for the perfect opportunity to strike. Once the target location was set, we'd move in and take them out. We had been doing it so long we'd started to think of it as a frustrating campaign of whack-a-mole. Each time we cut the head off of a bomb cell, another leader popped up. We weren't stopping the insurgency; we were just killing it off in parts. An insurgency doesn't have to win. It just has to survive.

I cared only about practical matters—the safety of my team, the number of expected enemy fighters, our route in and out. By this time we had plenty of practice playing the game, and a change in the pattern like this one was a major red flag for us all. The thirty thousand–foot strategy mattered little to me when I was eyeing a target. The strategy stuff was for the admirals and the politicians, not for the men on the ground.

Our theater commander decided we would hit the house. He was an Army Ranger colonel on a three-month rotation, and he saw the chance to kill or capture a high-level al Qaeda commander.

"He wants to check the 'killed an AQ commander' box so he can be a general," Scott joked. "Go get 'em, boys, right?"

At the time, I was upset by the order. Taking down a high-ranking commander with a unit under his command always looked good. But I suspect the Ranger colonel could read the pattern as well as we could, and just wanted to be certain an al Qaeda commander wasn't there. We were all fighting the same enemy, and he was doing what he thought needed to be done. It's extremely hard not to get emotional in situations like this, especially when people don't trust you and the stakes are so high.

As I matured through my career, I learned communication was one of the most important things I could provide to leaders and subordinates alike.

Our troop commander did his best to explain our issues with the mission to the Army colonel, but it didn't work. The troop commander was our highest-ranking officer. While the troop commander was important to our unit, he had likely just graduated from the training pipeline. The troop chief, on the other hand, had been with the command longer than the officer had even been in the Navy. The troop chief was the senior enlisted SEAL in the troop. He was pretty much the Mafia don, or the big cheese. Because experience is what matters most, it was the senior enlisted guys who ran the command.

Both the troop commander and the troop chief told the Ranger colonel we'd seen a few similar houses on previous deployments. The houses were rigged to explode when we arrived.

Because we shared Afghanistan with the Rangers, the commander in charge of the theater rotated every three months between a SEAL and a Ranger officer. It wasn't the perfect solution because culturally, SEALs and Rangers were on opposite ends of the spectrum, and so one side or the other was always trying to adapt to a commanding officer with a much different style than the troops were used to. We all had the same objectives, but the way we go about our business is vastly different.

The Army has certain institutional ways of doing things, just like the Navy. The difference can be boiled down pretty easily: Rangers think and plan from the top down. The SEALs think and plan from the bottom up.

Typically when we plan an assault, the enlisted team leaders and troop chiefs take the lead. We are trained to be free thinkers, not robots. The Rangers were very much the opposite. The Ranger commander would say, "I want to hit that target tonight," while a SEAL commander might say, "OK, guys, what do you think? Is this a target worth hitting tonight?"

Every guy in my squadron had been in the SEAL community a minimum of five years. Our guys were older and much more experienced, and we'd built trust both up and down our chain of command through years of combat.

Of course, the Rangers were also deploying and growing their combat experience, but they were typically much younger. Most of the Rangers were twenty years old or younger, compared to the average age of about thirty-one years old for the SEAL team.

The biggest difference was trust, and it hadn't been established at this point.

My team considered the target and its mysterious stationary cell phone signal, and it didn't add up. Our instinct was to continue to monitor the target before conducting a raid. There wasn't any significant movement on the target at all. But nothing we said resonated with the Ranger colonel. It seemed like he didn't trust us to make the call, even though we felt like we'd earned it. The order came down from the colonel to launch and conduct the raid.

"Fucking sweet, another armchair quarterback telling us what to do from miles away," one of the team leaders said.

"Well, at least it's not life or death," I said with a smirk as I walked out of the room.

At that moment, any trust we had in the Ranger colonel was gone. He wasn't listening to what we had to say. Any logical argument we made to wait and monitor the target for additional time was dismissed.

We gathered in the operations center to go over the plan one more time. Usually when we got missions, there was a little excitement. We joked that deployments were like minimum-security prison sentences because you were stuck in a camp and served the same shitty food that convicts ate back in the States, and you couldn't leave the wire without orders. Anytime we got to leave the wire it was better than sitting around camp, even if it meant you could get shot.

When I got to the operations center for the final brief, it felt like a cloud hung over this mission. I figured at best this was a dry hole and a waste of time. At worst, it was a setup and we were headed into an ambush.

"OK, boys," the troop chief said. "We're going to land on the Y instead of patrolling to the compound. Our hope is that the noise will stir up some commotion inside the compound and we'll actually be able to see some signs of life."

"Landing on the Y" meant that we would take a helicopter in to a spot near the target, just outside of RPG range. Instead of landing outside of earshot and sneaking in, we were hoping that the noise of the helicopters would spook the people in the house, causing them to run.

Of course, even if we did detect movement, it didn't mean

there wasn't a chance that the people on the target weren't all wearing suicide vests. We weren't too thrilled with the plan, but we didn't have much choice.

"This is the world we live in, this is our job, and we're going to do everything within our capabilities to make sure we do this right and that nobody gets hurt," the troop chief said.

I've heard one of my SEAL mentors say that there are rules about bitching. He said everyone has the right to bitch about a mission or job for five minutes. After those five minutes, you shut the fuck up and get to work. We got the full five minutes before we rode out to the helicopters in two small buses.

I didn't have time to dwell on the commander's decision as the bus bounced along the gravel road leading to the flight line. I wasn't thinking about the Ranger colonel. I wasn't thinking about how I was pissed that he was making us do this and putting us in a shitty position. I simply tried to focus on my three-foot world. My job wasn't to complain; my job was to clear that compound under the orders we were given. We could talk smack about the colonel's bad decision once we survived the mission; get distracted by it now, and we might not.

I sat cradling my suppressed HK MP7 in my lap. On my side, I was carrying a cut-down M79 grenade launcher. Our armorers had cut the barrels down shorter, cut the butt stock down into a pistol grip, and attached small red dot sights on top for more accuracy. I would always carry the M79, or "pirate gun," when I carried the lighter and less lethal MP7. If I had to engage any enemy past one hundred and fifty meters, I would have to use my M79.

All my gear was desert digital camouflage, or, as we call it, AOR1. My OCD tendencies required me to color coordinate everything. I'd learned my lesson with the parachute jump gone wrong years before. I'd been worried about bad-fitting gear and not focused on the jump. Tonight, all these years later, my gear felt like it was part of me. Tight, clean, streamlined.

Sitting across from me in the helicopter, the snipers had collapsible ladders at their feet. The ladders allowed them to climb the walls surrounding the compound and provide covering fire. Everything was set. We were ready. I just hoped as we landed that I'd hear reports from the drones flying overhead that they were seeing movement on the target.

I could hear the engines whine as we started to land. The ramp was already open as all of us anxiously waited for the helicopter to come to a stop. We jerked to a halt as the wheels touched down and settled into a huge cloud of dust. The troop chief and troop commander were both on the radio with the drone circling above.

"Negative movement," I heard the troop chief say over the team net. "I repeat, no movement on target."

Either the Taliban had learned some serious discipline or no one was home, I thought as I raced down the ramp.

My mind was pinging as I followed my teammates off the bird. I was ready for a fight. I half hoped and half expected to hear the familiar rattle of AK-47 fire or the whoosh of an

RPG. Once I cleared the dust cloud from the helicopter's rotors, I took a knee and waited.

We formed a large "L" around the compound and listened to the noise from the helicopter. There was nothing but silence as the last thump of the rotor faded. No one ran. There was no yelling. Everything we did was slow and methodical. There was no hurry.

Why rush to a gunfight or ambush?

There was little moonlight, but under our night vision goggles the area looked like a green moonscape. I could see the walls of the compound a couple hundred meters away. The ground was rutted, dry, and dusty. It didn't look like any farmer had touched the field in a while. My eyes traced the compound's wall to the corner and then tracked into the wood line nearby. We often found fighters in the trees, but none of the drones spotted anyone either before we arrived or after the helicopters departed. I half expected to find the fighters holed up outside waiting to ambush us as we hit the house. If this were a legit target, the al Qaeda commander's bodyguards would definitely be nearby.

From above us, the drones still weren't seeing any movement. The only activity was two heat sources—people, likely men—standing on a rooftop that was well over five hundred meters away. The men could have simply been innocent farmers awakened by the noise of our helicopters, or they could be spotters for a possible ambush.

I watched as our snipers out front slowly crept across the field toward the compound walls. They got to the base of the wall, extended their ladders, and climbed up into their over-watch positions. From the snipers' vantage point, they could see inside the walls and cover us as we approached.

We held our position until one by one, all the snipers checked in over the radio. They all had the same report: "Negative movement in the compound."

"Snipers, good copy," I heard the troop chief say over the net. "Assault element, commence assault."

I was part of the assault team and near the front of the formation. I could see Scott in front of me. Slowly, I started to move toward the compound. I picked my way over the loose dirt and massive rocks.

"Still no movement," the troop chief said as he relayed information from the drones and snipers.

When I got to the wall, I followed my teammates around to the front of the compound. Scott got to the gate first. As I closed in behind him, I could see that the gate had actually been left open just a small amount, just enough to be inviting. The only thing missing at this point was the welcome mat laid out in front for us to wipe our feet on before we entered.

Scott searched around the gate for booby traps. He looked quickly around the courtyard to make sure no one was waiting and then slowly pushed the gate open a bit further, constantly scanning the courtyard.

There was no reason for talking, let alone some crazy commando hand and arm signals. We'd all worked together for so long, we knew Scott was working his magic, and when he was ready he would let us know. He finally waved us forward and we lightly stepped over the doorjamb and into the compound.

I brushed by him and entered the courtyard. Just inside the gate to the left were two doorways leading into the small one-story main house. An animal pen was on the right side of the compound and in the far corner. It was empty.

I crossed the courtyard and followed my teammates toward the house. Ahead of me, one of my teammates was pushing in the wooden door of the first room. I could see the light spilling out of the room as I moved toward the second door.

"If they have lights on, that must be a good sign," I thought. Typically that meant someone was home. Not many houses in Afghanistan have electricity, let alone enough to leave the lights on when no one is around.

I stopped at the second door and waited for a squeeze from one of my teammates confirming he was behind me.

"Take it," my teammate whispered, squeezing my shoulder.

Using my left hand, I slowly opened the wooden door. It was stuck on its old hinges and let out a loud creak as I pushed it open. The house smelled of dust and not the usual Afghan potpourri of animal dung and cooking oil. The room was completely dark.

Before entering the room I scanned for any movement. The room was empty. Most Afghan houses are full of junk strewn everywhere. There is always stuff—blankets, crates full of rusted parts, used cans of cooking oil—in every room you enter. This room was completely empty except for a piece of cardboard in the center of the floor.

I wasn't sure it was cardboard at first. It was hard to tell through my night vision goggles. It just seemed out of place, especially since it was such a new piece of cardboard. It's very rare that you ever see anything new in Afghanistan, so seeing what seemed to be a brand-new, clean piece of cardboard in an empty room was a huge red flag.

"Hold up," I whispered to my teammates behind me.

I reached down and picked up one edge. The cardboard was covering some sort of hole. I could see the edges as I picked the cardboard up a little more. It was hard to see in the hole. A sharp fin caught my eye and I followed it down to the fat body of a bomb.

The bomb was gray with American warnings and markings. The hole in the floor was deep enough that the fins at the back of the bomb were flush with the floor. I let the cardboard go and moved back from the hole.

Before I could say anything or even warn my teammates, I heard someone outside in the main courtyard start yelling.

I was milliseconds from calling myself after spotting the bomb under the cardboard. For all I knew, the bomb was rigged to blow remotely.

I found out later that my teammates in the first room with the light on had entered another empty room. A single lightbulb hung from the ceiling. Directly under the light was a rug on the floor. Centered on the rug were two RPG rockets lying in an "X."

At about the same time I discovered the bomb, they found the RPG rockets.

We'd been set up.

Behind me I could see my teammates heading for the main gate of the compound. As silent and slow as we were coming in, we were the opposite getting out.

Scott was still at the gate when I arrived. He'd stayed there to pull security when he saw a pair of wires running from the gate into the ground. The gate was rigged to explode if it was opened fully. I was glad he'd inched it open only as far as he needed to. The gate confirmed what we knew already.

The phone.

The rockets.

The gate.

The compound was one massive bomb set to explode when we arrived.

Scott started the call when he saw the wires attached to the back side of the gate. He didn't want the gate left unattended because someone could have inadvertently triggered the bomb. As each assaulter sprinted past him and out of the compound, he very carefully controlled the door to keep it in the safest position possible.

I carefully squeezed through the open door and broke into a dead sprint into the nearby field. I don't think I'd ever run that fast in my life. It was the speed of fright. I made it back to where we got off the helicopters and took a knee near a small ditch. My mouth was completely dry, and I took a pull off my CamelBak, spitting a mouthful of water into the dirt. Scott stayed in place directing traffic until everyone had exited the compound. He was the last one to carefully step through the gate and begin his sprint away from the compound.

"I need a head count," the troop chief said as he worked his way down the line.

I was part of Alpha team. I could see my team leader moving around trying to identify every member of the team. We all looked the same through night vision, so I trotted over and checked in with him. He gave me the thumbs-up and walked over to the troop chief.

"Alpha is up," my team leader said.

I went back to my spot in a shallow ditch. The radio came to life again and I could hear the chatter as the troop commander and troop chief started working on approvals for an air strike with our joint terminal attack controller (JTAC).

Overhead, two A-10 attack fighters were circling. I could hear the faint crack of their engines as they got lined up to bomb the compound. The JTAC was talking them in, giving the pilots the compound's location and landmarks to make sure the bombs hit the intended target.

Our only course of action was to blow the bombs in place. It was too dangerous to try to disarm them. The house was deserted and there would be no collateral damage. The other houses were too far away, meaning any women or children or other innocents in the area were safe.

"Bombs away, ten seconds," I heard our JTAC report over the radio.

We passed the warning down the line. Lying as low as I could in the ditch, I wasn't yet focused on how close we had all come to dying. All I could think about was how I really hoped the Ranger colonel learned his lesson.

"Five seconds."

We were lying flat on our stomachs and trying to make ourselves as small as possible because we were still relatively close to the target. The unmistakable shriek of the A-10 engines grew louder. Even with my helmet on and my face buried as deep as I could get it in the ditch, the pitch-black night sky lit up as the compound exploded in a huge fireball. Seconds later, the explosion from two five-hundred-pound laser-guided bombs echoed back through the valley. Behind me, the A-10s banked and climbed as the thunder of the explosion faded.

I started to rise from my position of cover when another fireball mushroomed out from what was left of the walls of the compound. The bomb rigged to kill us had cooked off, sending debris arcing out of the middle of the compound.

Chunks of mud and rock landed with a "thunk" in the dirt around us. I slithered back into the ditch, trying to keep my head low. I felt something poke my thigh and I shifted my weight. At first I thought I'd rolled onto a sticker bush or thorn, but something was still sticking me in the leg. I inched up out of my position slowly and checked the ditch for a sticker bush, but there was nothing but dirt. I rubbed the spot where I was poked and felt it again.

I slid my gloved hand into my pocket and pulled out a shard of shrapnel. It was no bigger than a dime. Shaped like a dagger, it had a jagged edge that was stabbing me in the leg. The metal was so hot that it had melted the foam earplugs that I always stowed in my left pocket. I rolled the shard of shrapnel between my fingers after it cooled. I had no idea how it got into my pocket, but I was damn lucky it wasn't bigger or hadn't been moving faster when it hit me.

"That was some shit," I heard a teammate say as we started to walk back to the landing zone. "I'd love to be there when the troop commander tells the colonel 'I told you so.'"

I felt the same way. We were all angry. The Ranger colonel should have trusted us to make an assessment. We should have delayed the operation for a day and collected more intelligence. We knew the targeted phone was on and not moving. Why did we need to rush to hit the compound? We call this "tactical patience," and the Ranger colonel was obviously in short supply.

The helicopter ride back was long. I could see my teammates seething in the seats around me. It was too loud to talk, but our body language gave away our anger. No one liked the mission from the start. We'd voiced our concerns, and they'd fallen on deaf ears. The officer who had ordered the raid had probably watched it from his desk back at a base hundreds of miles away, while we went into harm's way.

I have learned over and over again in the SEALs that trust is the bedrock of any relationship. Our commanders had to trust us to execute our mission, but on the flip side they needed to trust us when we saw something wrong. It has to flow both ways or it doesn't work. I knew as I walked off the ramp of the helicopter, I'd never trust another order from this particular Ranger colonel.

After the mission, we took a lot of time going over the concerns we had voiced before the mission. Of course, the Ranger commander wasn't present. He was back at his headquarters in Bagram. One of the hardest lessons I had to learn from my younger days as a SEAL was to avoid becoming too emotional, even if we knew we were right. I remember several times during the AAR for that mission having to consciously tell myself to be calm as we talked through every aspect of the planning and actions on the objective.

As we talked, I rolled the piece of shrapnel between my fingers. It was a reminder of more than my luck. It reminded me that we very easily could have been killed because an inexperienced Army colonel didn't want to listen to his subject-matter experts.

"So what the fuck are we going to do about this?" one of my teammates blurted out during the AAR.

"Seriously, he could have killed us," said another.

Finally our troop chief spoke up.

"OK, guys, I know we're all pretty worked up right now," the troop chief said. "We're all very emotional, as we should be. But we're going to collect up everyone's lessons learned and sit on it for a day or two."

The troop chief was right; there was no reason to go running back to the Ranger colonel bitching and moaning about how he almost got us killed. Being too emotional only undercuts a message that would be more effective after we'd cooled down. It is unlikely he would have been receptive if we came back and complained in an unprofessional manner.

Several days later, our troop commander had the pleasure of calling the Ranger colonel and explaining, in detail and as politely and coldly as he was capable of, why the decision he made to assault that target was ill advised. By waiting and taking the emotion out of it, the troop commander was able to get the point across. If nothing else was accomplished, it showed the colonel that he would always get our honest assessment of a mission, and it also showed that we could be trusted to make an accurate assessment of a target. This communication was a chance for our troop leadership to begin to build trust with the colonel. Of course, we were all still worked up and pissed, but this wasn't our leadership's first rodeo. I can remember being impressed that my troop chief and commander were so composed. They had already learned that running back with an emotional outburst wasn't going to help anybody. Instead, their calm demeanor, honest feedback, and clear communication were vital to building trust. I was impressed how they treated the colonel the same way they treated the junior SEALs in the troop. This was a skill I would struggle to learn throughout my career, at least being able to be unemotional about it.

Trust is one of those tricky things that can't be bought by rank or title. It has to be earned through trial and error, through shared experience, and through constant communication. The Ranger colonel had lost my trust in that mission and would definitely have to earn it back. Hopefully, through our leadership's response and feedback he would now trust our troop next time we had an issue with an operation. Of course, the trust I had in Scott and in all of my teammates only grew stronger.

CHAPTER 7

After Action Review

Communication

I stifled a long yawn as I walked back to our ready room and took off my kit, which was soaked with dust and sweat. I was tired, having come down from the adrenaline of combat, and feeling the sting of missing the target.

We gathered in the briefing room near our operations center in eastern Afghanistan. It was summer 2010. The heat was oppressive, requiring us to haul extra water on every mission. The good thing was I drank most of it, so by the time the mission ended my load was lighter.

I could just make out the sun peeking over the mountains. It had been a long night and I knew tonight's After Action Review, which we call the AAR for short, was going to be tough.

We'd been tracking a Taliban commander just north of Khost. The valley was one of several sanctuaries where they cached weapons and explosives. We started tracking them via ISR, which is shorthand for intelligence, surveillance, and reconnaissance, which is what we call drones. When they finally stopped moving from village to village and settled into a network of compounds at the end of the valley, we launched.

But after landing just out of RPG range of the compounds, we got several reports of squirters running from the target. We chased them for several hours, but the target got away. Back at the base, I knew there were going to be a lot of very direct questions about what the fuck happened and why the enemy had gotten away. We want to do our job as clean and as perfect as we can, but the rules of engagement kept us boxed in and we lost our target. It was one thing to hit a dry hole, but this time we knew the guy was there and failed to kill or capture him. We don't put our lives on the line to fail.

Frankly, at the end of a long mission, when you're fried, frustrated, and angry about failing, sitting down and talking it out is often the last thing you want to do. But I had seen the AAR work throughout my career and I knew it was a vital part of our culture.

The AAR is one of the ways we fix mistakes. It was a time to ask questions and make sure we were doing the job right. AARs can get emotional, frustrating, long-winded, and even boring, but no matter what people think of them, they are absolutely critical.

I thought we had made the right call given the situation on the ground and the rules of engagement. We'd all agreed that landing on the "Y" for this operation was the right choice, but we had obviously been wrong. No matter how bad egos might get bruised, it was important to explore every reason why our operation had failed. We needed to fix our failure, and the most important AARs are the hard ones. Imagine if the military hadn't held an AAR after Operation Eagle Claw, the botched raid in 1980 to free the American hostages in Iran.

The investigation that followed that failed operation pointed out gaps in the military mission planning, from a lack of cohesion between services to a need for better equipment. It was specifically because of that failure that ▮▮▮ has become as successful as it is today.

An AAR is a place where lessons are learned and policies are modified or scrapped, all with an eye toward making the team better. This type of dialogue ensures buy-in from both the top and bottom of the chain of command. The key is that we get as many players in the room as possible. The only way an AAR works is if everyone leaves their ego outside and comes in willing to take honest criticism.

On the way into the meeting, I ran into my buddy Walt. No taller than my armpit, Walt was short, but his attitude, cocky with a swagger, compensated for it. He had a healthy dose of little-man syndrome and an inordinate amount of body hair. He was one of my best friends and always a straight shooter when it came to voicing his opinion.

Walt was covered in mud from head to foot. The mud was so thick it was impossible to run a comb through his beard. I smiled when I saw him. He just shook his head, letting a small smirk crease his lips. I could make out his white teeth peeking out of the mound of matted hair tangled beneath his chin.

"Not a fucking word," he said. "That was bullshit. We need to figure this shit out. We can't keep flying in and giving away our position. Especially if they aren't going to let us drop bombs."

The Taliban commanders must have heard the rotor wash echoing off the valley walls a few minutes before we landed. It was like an early-warning system. When they heard helicopters, they ran.

Walt and his teammates had tried to catch the fighters after they ran from the compounds but lost them in the mountains. As we walked into the briefing, everyone looked dejected, angry, and frustrated. No two SEALs in the room looked the same. We each wore different, usually mismatched uniforms; some operators wore beards; some had long hair. We all had a drink of some sort—coffee, water, Rip It energy drinks. This was going to be a long talk.

Walt and I sat down in two of the chairs in the room. We were joined by one of Walt's teammates, who wore a black Van Halen T-shirt instead of his camouflage shirt. The white Van Halen logo was bright and clean because it had been covered by his body armor. Like Walt, he was covered everywhere else with mud.

"That's a good look for you," I said with a smile.

He didn't return the smile.

None of us wanted to risk death only to fail. If we were going to do our jobs, we had to find a way to work within the rules of engagement because the Taliban knew the rules, too, and used them against us. The Taliban knew that if they dropped their guns and ran that we couldn't just shoot them. They knew if they blended in with the civilian population they could slip away. If it were just a matter of dropping bombs or shooting the guys we knew were bad, the war would have been much easier. That being said, that's not what we're about, and none of us were about to shoot unarmed people. Besides, if we even remotely got out of line, what seemed like thirty different lawyers all working for the officers up the food chain would tell us all about it.

Shit, by my last deployment we were barely even allowed to enter a structure or building in Afghanistan without prior approval from higher up. It made fighting the war almost impossible.

Walt and I were some of the last ones into the AAR. Before it started, I took a minute to focus and calm down. I let the frustration of watching the fighters escape bleed away. Emotion had no place in an AAR. It got in the way of good communication. I took two deep breaths and pushed the thoughts of failure out of my mind. I'd become adept at compartmentalizing things, and I knew I needed a clear head for this conversation.

Taped to the side of the tent wall was a poster-size piece of paper with the checklist for the AAR.

Mission Planning

Infil

Actions on the Objective

TQ [Tactical Questioning]

Exfil

Comms [Communications]

Intel

HQ

Each of us took turns talking about our role in the mission. As a team leader, I would start by speaking for my team, and my guys would jump in if they had something to add. Everyone was not only free to talk, but encouraged to speak up.

The troop chief started things off by going over the mission planning. From there, we started talking through each part of the operation, starting with the infil. We came in on two CH-47 helicopters, using the infil strategy called "flying to the Y."

Flying to the Y had been no different than previous missions. The radio exploded with chatter about squirters as soon as we started to land. I was right behind my point man as we dashed off the ramp, peeling to the far-right flank of our formation to get a good angle on the compounds.

Over the radio, I heard Steve, Walt's team leader, roger up to pursue the fighters. They followed the drone's laser marker past the buildings and into the hills. I waited for the word to start the assault toward the compounds. Individual teams immediately started peeling off to take flanking positions and provide a base of fire.

"OK," said the troop chief over the radio. "Let's take it."

We started toward the target. I saw other teams and Afghan commandos disappear into a maze of compounds. My team surrounded one building and stopped. We set up at the door and tried the latch. It was unlocked. The point man pushed the door open.

The house was pitch-black, but we could see pretty well with our night vision goggles. The house had one main room with a kitchen in one corner. The place was deserted. There were no fighters. No weapons. No explosives. Nothing.

Outside, I saw a few Afghan commandos standing guard over some women and children. Over the radio, Steve was still racing after the fleeing fighters. I could see the drone's laser tracking the Taliban fighters far up the hill. Well behind them were Steve and his team. I could see the IR strobes on their helmets blinking. They were cutting a zigzag up the hill trying to catch up.

"That sucks," I said to a teammate watching them with me. "That looks miserable. Hope they catch 'em."

Over the radio, Steve was asking for close air support. He wanted the AC-130 gunship to open fire, but he couldn't get approval. Finally, after more than an hour chasing the fighters up the side of the mountain and deeper into unknown territory, the troop commander and troop chief called the mission. There was no use in continuing to pursue the fighters, especially since our team wasn't gaining any ground on them and they weren't getting approval to drop bombs.

The troop commander called for exfil and the first helicopter landed near the network of compounds. We walked up the ramp and slumped into the orange jump seats. Seconds later, I could feel the helicopter lift off and head back to the base.

The other helicopter headed for Steve's team, including Walt. They were too far away to walk back and we didn't have the time to sit and wait as they scaled back down the mountain. These were not rolling hills either. We were talking mountains, ones with snowcaps in the winter. A helicopter exfil at Steve's location wasn't going to be easy.

Steve and his team needed one hand on the mountain at all times as they waited for the helicopter to arrive. The twin-rotor CH-47 helicopter couldn't land, so the pilot from the 160th Special Operations Aviation Regiment flew past the cliff, stopped in a hover, and slowly backed the open ramp to the edge of the rocks. The rotors were within a few feet of the rock face. The 160th pilots were the best in the world. Only these pilots could have pulled this type of exfil off. Steve's team watched the pilots back the bus-size helicopter to the cliff face. The downdraft from the spinning rotor blades kicked up dirt and debris that showered the SEALs with rocks and coated their uniforms in mud.

The pilots maneuvered the helicopter's ramp to within a few feet of the cliff. One by one, Steve and his team jumped from the rocks to the ramp.

"Man, you guys would still be making your way down that mountain if the pilots hadn't pulled off that exfil," I said to Walt as he described leaping for the ramp.

"We were getting blasted by rocks for at least five minutes," Walt said. "I'm not sure what would have been worse, the walk back down the mountain or the welts I have all over my body."

"Maybe the Van Halen shirt jinxed you," one of the other SEALs said.

"Yeah, Walt, maybe the weight of your mud-covered beard slowed you down," I said.

It was funny to us because we weren't the ones who had to climb the mountain. We were having a good laugh about Steve and his team, but they weren't enjoying the joke. They'd tried their best to get the fighters and felt let down when the air strikes weren't approved.

"Why did we do this?" Walt finally asked. "These tactics aren't working. I can't believe I humped around the side of a mountain and we didn't even get the guy."

Finally, Steve chimed in about not getting approval to use the AC-130.

"What is the point of having Spectre on target if they can't shoot?" Steve said. "Was there any question these assholes were bad?"

Steve already knew the answer.

There was no question the squirters were bad. But, under the rules of engagement, we had to see the guns. And while the drones tracked the fighters, it wasn't clear if they were armed. I didn't have any doubt. Neither did my teammates. But we weren't the ones giving approval.

"These guys got away because of the way we planned the

target," Steve finally said. "Our guys were smoked and these two knuckleheads should have been captured or smoke checked."

The Taliban learned from the mujahedeen's fight against the Soviets. They picked areas to hide that were difficult to reach, except by helicopter. We often had no choice but to fly to the Y.

"Guys, we made the decision to land on the Y because of the terrain surrounding the target," the troop chief said. "We knew the risks going in that there was a chance the enemy could spook and haul ass."

It was becoming hard for us to justify ever landing on the Y because as soon as the fighters heard you coming, which was a few minutes before you actually landed, they started squirting or hauling ass away from the target. The only way it worked was when we could get containment on the target and block all the escape routes. If you aren't on the ground ahead of the helicopters, all bets are off. You're going to spend the night chasing squirters.

We preferred to patrol into targets. It allowed us to keep the element of surprise and set up around the target to keep fighters from fleeing when the shooting started. I looked over at the recce team leader. His team planned the routes and set up snipers on target.

"The routes into that specific valley are very limited, and the patrol would have been hard as hell, if we could even keep our timeline at that," the recce team leader said.

It would have taken us six hours to walk up the valley and

over the mountain peaks. The recce guys weren't sure we could make the timeline. Especially with the number of assaulters we needed to bring on the target. We had to take the Afghan commandos, our partner force, and two members from the conventional Army unit responsible for the valley.

There was no doubt in anybody's mind that neither the Afghan commandos nor the Army guys could have made the patrol. Let alone on the faster timeline that we would need in order to reach the target in time.

Each year, since the beginning of the war, the rules of engagement had changed to match the political winds. At the time of this mission, partnering with the Afghans was the order of the day. A mission once reserved for the Special Forces was now getting farmed out to every unit from paratroopers to regular SEAL teams. We were being required to bring along Afghan commandos who couldn't speak English and wouldn't last two minutes in BUD/S. The Afghan commandos, on paper, were Afghanistan's answer to our counterterror units. But in reality, the troops were only a slight upgrade from the regular Afghan soldiers running around the country.

We also had to bring along a herd of other stragglers or enablers, like "battle space owners," or BSOs, so they could witness the operation. These were American military soldiers stationed near the target. If the elders from the village came down to the nearest base to complain and accuse us of killing innocent farmers, the Army guys would be able to say they witnessed everything and defuse the situation.

It made doing our simple things even harder. On several occasions because of weight restrictions on the helicopters, we bumped SEALs off the helicopter and the mission just to make room for an Afghan commando or a conventional Army BSO.

"These BSOs and Afghan commandos just aren't useful at all," I said. "Is there any way we can talk to the higher-ups and explain to them how limiting they are to our mission?"

The troop chief almost laughed.

"You've been here long enough to know that this is what we're stuck with," he said. "This is the hand we've been dealt and we have to play it."

I shook my head and took a drink of my coffee. I did know the answer, but it felt good to say it. At least if we threw it on the table, the team could debate it or at least know dumping everyone who wasn't a SEAL from the mission was considered.

The AAR was spinning. If we tried to patrol in with our entire gaggle of people, we knew we wouldn't make it. If we used helicopters and landed on the Y, we knew we'd spook the fighters and they'd leave. The troop chief finally jumped in and got us back on track. Nobody was specifically to blame in this AAR other than ourselves. No one person ordered us to land on the Y. We were all more pissed at the limitations of the rules of engagement, or ROE, as well as the fact that our target got away. As we went round and round, people began getting louder and louder and more and more intense. Pretty soon the whole AAR was breaking down and there were more emotions than cold hard facts or new ideas.

"Look, guys, we have rules," the troop chief said. "We didn't write them, but we have to follow them. The key here is that we've discussed everything that happened right and everything that happened wrong. We take on board every single lesson we've learned and we don't make the same mistakes twice."

I looked around the room, and some of the guys were nodding. I agreed with the troop chief. We couldn't go back in time and fix anything.

"The fact of the matter is we have to find a better way to hit these compounds," the troop chief said. "These guys knew what they were doing. They ran when they heard the helicopters. Everybody needs to reflect on that fact for a minute. Stop pointing fingers at your teammates or at the rules of engagement and start focusing on the big picture. We took a swing and it didn't work. Let's figure out a better way next time."

The AAR got the issues out in the open and forced us to think outside of the box and communicate. We still needed to find a way to do an offset infil with all the extra people we were required to take on a mission.

In the end, the AAR eliminated any infighting. Everyone had a chance to say their piece and air any concerns. It allowed us all to openly communicate. Frustrations were aired in that room and hopefully in that room only. Nobody carried on later because we all knew that this was the place and setting to let our voices be heard. Just the chance to communicate, with no sugarcoating, with no rank, and with complete openness and honestly, was what we needed to correct both big and small problems.

I remember a particularly uncomfortable and very personal AAR after I became a team leader. It was in Afghanistan and it was shortly after Phil, my old team leader, was shot in the leg. We were in the middle of the deployment, so I wasn't expecting to take over the team leader responsibilities until the following deployment. I was still getting used to having the added responsibility. Since I was a new team leader, I didn't want to screw anything up. I knew my troop chief would be watching me closely. Luckily my entire eight-man team was more talented than I was and made being a first-time team leader much easier.

The target, as usual, was a Taliban commander or facilitator. We'd tracked him to a bed-down location in a village near the Pakistan border. After we raided the compound and captured him, our troop chief put out the word to prepare for exfil.

We all have our standard kit—weapons, night vision, body armor—plus we had additional gear like ladders and sledgehammers to breach doors. Every member of the team is assigned extra gear. I carried a set of bolt cutters on my back. I don't know how many times someone would use them and set them down instead of returning the bolt cutters to me. This happened routinely with all the extra equipment that we would carry on a mission. When it came time to leave the target, I wouldn't have all of the equipment that I was responsible for.

Everybody was getting ready to leave. It was night and pitch-black and I wanted to make sure that everybody had

Starting a fire during the winter growing up in Alaska. I always carried the beaver-skin fur hat my mom made for me on my coldest deployments.

Meeting my first SEAL. Notice my sweet SEAL shirt, which I promptly took off and never wore again.

My swim buddy and me in our hotel room waiting for the call to go board the U-Haul. Taken during the Ketchikan exercise.

Divers and safety boat off the pier in Ketchikan, Alaska, a short distance from where a killer whale had had its breakfast that morning.

Me during my first HAHO, or high-altitude high-opening, jump trip with my ST6 squadron, just before my parachute cutaway.

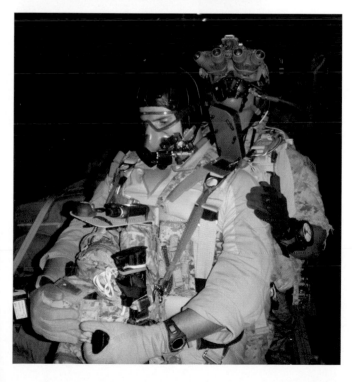

A tandem jump during a training evolution. HAHO jumps require oxygen, and at night NODs are mandatory.

Epic fail! If you look close, you can see the skid marks on the ground behind me.

Hair Missile and handler on an Afghanistan deployment.

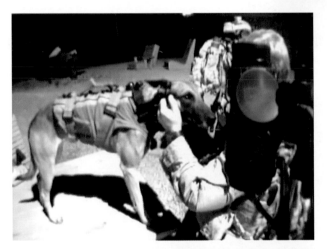

Hair Missile during one of our missions in Iraq.

Training off the coast of Virginia. Most units never have assets like this. We had a "big deck" aircraft carrier and a TF 160 helicopter.

Me running and gunning during some training when I was at ST5.

Training with our four-by-fours and side by sides.

Afghanistan. The MiG is a reminder of when Russia fought there for years as well.

Afghan partner forces.

A buddy and me about to head out on a freezing-cold winter mission in a snow-swept valley.

Me and my MP7 flying home from the mission with the house rigged to blow.

The Delta guys and me after we almost landed on the wrong house.

My team just before the mission in the Evolution chapter. Always watch the shoes!

Phil and me taking a break before some training. Phil is not only a good friend but a mentor.

The morning after the rescue of Captain Phillips.

An Emerson Knife that I carried on the UBL raid and donated to charity. The money raised went to a fallen teammate's family.

Me trading books with Gene Wentz, the author of *Men in Green Faces*. It was the first SEAL book I read, and it set me on my track to become one.

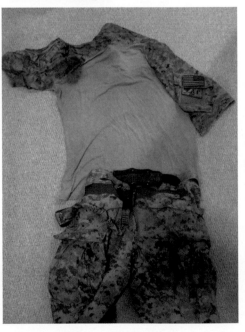

My camo uniform when I returned from the UBL raid. The blood on the upper left is where the bullet frag entered my shoulder.

their stuff. We were lining up to patrol back to the landing zone, and I got on the radio net monitored by my whole team and called Jake, call sign Alpha Eight.

Jake had the ladder for our team, and I wanted to make sure he didn't forget it. But I used a frequency that everyone could hear.

"Alpha Eight, this is Alpha One," I said.

"Alpha One, this is Eight, go ahead," he said.

"Hey, you got your ladder?" I said.

"Roger that," he replied almost immediately.

From there, I double-checked that I had a good head count for my team, then called the troop chief.

"Echo Twelve, Alpha One. Alpha is ready to exfil."

Each team leader quickly checked in with the same, but none of them went to the extent of asking their individual guys if they had their extra gear.

"Roger, recce take us out," the troop chief said.

Back at the base we immediately dropped our gear and sat down for the AAR. As we ended the exfil portion of our AAR, Jake raised his hand.

"Hey, just curious why you had to get on the radio and remind me about my ladder?"

"What do you mean?" I said.

"Well, it's my gear, it's my responsibility," Jake said. "I've never forgotten it before."

At first I was a bit taken back. I really didn't know what to say. I was the team leader and I had the right to ask him anything I wanted. I could have gotten on the radio and asked him his shoe size or if he brushed his teeth that morning. But then it clicked. Instantly, I felt like an ass.

"Good point," I said.

I sat there in front of the whole team, feeling like an asshole. I was so concerned about my team doing things correctly that I wasn't paying attention to my own behavior. I'd become the team leader that I'd always hated, the micromanager. Sure, in the back of my mind I'd rationalized asking him about the ladder because it was a big piece of equipment that I wanted to make sure we didn't forget on target. But what I didn't do was trust my guy to be responsible for his own gear. Phil was always really good at letting us do our own thing. He trusted us to do our jobs and spoke up only when he had to correct you. I knew I had fucked up if Phil had to come talk to me. Otherwise, we were expected to know what we had to do. I'd wasted my breath and energy asking Jake about the ladder. Now I had to answer for my mistake during the AAR.

"Did I remind you to bring your bolt cutters or even your gun tonight?" Jake asked me.

"No," I said.

"Well, the ladder is my gear, it's my responsibility, so I've got it."

Of course he knew what gear to carry. The way I'd asked sounded like I didn't trust my teammates, and we all understood the importance of trust.

"My mistake," I said. "Good copy, roger that. I'm an ass and I get what you're saying. It won't happen again."

I was never mad at Jake. I was embarrassed and mad at myself.

All the credit goes to Jake. He knew that the AAR was the perfect time to bring up my error. Had Jake not been honest enough to communicate with me directly, I probably would have done the same thing the very next mission and it would have become habit.

Both the ladder AAR and the one after the mission when we lost the Taliban commander served the purpose.

The day after the failed mission to capture the Taliban commander, we were out on a new target. There wasn't time to dwell on the past. We all blocked out the last mission because we had to go back into harm's way, as a team, without second-guessing the men to our left and right.

But a month later, the troop chief came back to us with the same target.

"You guys want to take another swing at these guys?" the troop chief asked.

"Yeah," I said. "Of course."

I was in the operation center with Steve. The troop chief was there with the recce team leader. On the flat screen were satellite photos of the target compounds and the valley.

"He's back at home," the troop chief said, pointing to one of the compounds in the cluster. "Intel has him corralled to the exact same compound we hit before. He is there with a couple of buddies."

I looked at the compound and then looked at the valley as a whole. I wanted another shot. I'd let the first mission go and tried not to focus on the shithead getting away, but I wasn't about to let him pass through our fingers again.

"Your team has primary," the troop chief said to me.

My team could pick what we wanted to do on target.

"I want to walk in," I said.

I loved the harder stuff. If there was more of a challenge, I ate it up. The harder the mission, the more I liked it. But I also knew the obstacles we faced on this target. The AAR had shown us the problems with our first plan. We had to find a way to keep the element of surprise or it wasn't worth taking another swing at capturing or killing this guy.

I looked at the recce team leader. He had a smile on his face.

"I found a route," the recce team leader said. "But we can't do it with a big patrol."

"I agree. The last thing we need is that huge gaggle snaking its way through the mountains," I said. "There is no way we'd make it."

We'd learned a valuable lesson the last time. I thought back to the AAR and why we took the helicopters the first time.

"What about the commandos and battle space owners?" I asked. "Any way to get them in a different way?"

We talked for an hour and finally came up with a plan that fit with the rules of engagement. My team of SEALs, combined with our recce guys, an Air Force Pararescue Jumper (PJ) and our troop chief would take a helicopter to a nearby valley and patrol to the target. Once we had containment set around the network of compounds, we would radio back. The other teams plus the battle space owner and Afghan commandos would come in by helicopter and land on the Y. We'd already be in place to handle any squirters and to commence the assault as soon as the helos touched down. We finally had a work-around. It had been developed during the AAR.

We briefed the plan to the entire troop and grabbed our gear, and my team headed for the helicopters. We left hours before the main body and started to patrol. It was hot and we weren't a kilometer into the patrol before my shirt was soaked with sweat. There was little moon, and if I hadn't had my night vision it would have been impossible to see. For hours we walked up and down the hills.

The patrol was long but uneventful. I kept my focus, hoping all this hard work was going to pay off. The last thing I wanted was to let these fuckers get away again. We'd come up with a great plan and were now putting in the work to make it happen.

We finally crested the last hill and I could see the maze of compounds below. I checked my watch. We were on time. We quickly moved down and set up on the different alleys leading out of the small group of compounds. From the satellite images, we'd figured there were a couple of avenues out of the compound network. We split into teams of two and set up on each one.

We moved silently down the hill. I kept my rifle at the ready as we got close to the walls. I was with another SEAL, my swim buddy, and we took a knee and waited. Overhead, ISR was keeping track of the compounds. There were no reports of movers. When all the teams were in place, I heard the troop chief come over the radio.

"Birds are inbound," the troop chief said. "Two minutes."

I looked at my watch. I could already hear the faint thud of the rotors as the helicopters flew up the valley toward the compounds. I wiped the sweat off my face with my sleeve. If the fighters were indeed in the compound, I expected them to start running for it any minute.

Seconds later I heard the drone pilot over the radio.

"We've got two movers leaving the target compound and heading east," the drone pilot said.

That was all that I wanted to hear. We were set up to the east and ready and waiting for them.

I knew from the satellite images they were headed down a long alley that split the cluster of six compounds in half. It was the same route they used the first time we hit the compounds. At the end of the alley, Bert, who was one of my newer guys, and an Air Force PJ were set up.

"Coming your way, Alpha Four," I said over the radio.

"Roger," Bert said.

The rotors were loud now as the helicopter was landing on the western side of the compounds. I could just make them out in the cloud of dust. The radio crackled with reports as my teammates and the Afghan commandos fanned out and started moving toward the compounds.

Seconds later, I heard the crack of suppressed rifle fire as

Bert and the pararescueman opened up. The fighters—carrying AK-47s—got only a few steps out of the alley before running into Bert. The fighters were in a dead sprint. They looked up just as they cleared the alley and saw Bert and the PJ. The fighters tried to skid to a stop and raise their rifles in a weak-ass attempt to get some shots off. Before they even had a chance to level their AK-47s, Bert and the PJ fired multiple rounds into each fighter. They went down in a heap at the mouth of the alley.

"Two EKIA," Bert radioed.

Both fighters were killed in action. I felt instant gratification. We'd gotten them. We'd missed on the first try but didn't get discouraged. We'd talked through the failed mission—focused on what went right and what went wrong—and then found a new way to attack the target.

You don't often get a second chance in combat. We never counted on taking another swing at these guys, but we knew that the lessons learned from the first mission would help future missions.

The AAR served its purpose, and because of it, the two Taliban commanders would never be a threat again. We had figured out how to work around the requirements placed on us while still operating within the rules of engagement. This mission and the lessons learned had been pretty straightforward. However, many AARs and the lessons learned in them aren't so simple. Sometimes people die because we haven't clearly communicated and learned from our mistakes.

As hard as it can be to criticize the actions of a teammate, or to take criticism from a brother, it is one of the most important tools a SEAL has to improve. The hardest thing to do is honestly communicate with people, especially when you might be at fault. Mistakes are made in combat and that's understandable. The thing to remember is that communication and the lessons learned from the AAR are only put in place to make the team better. Understanding that it's not all about you is tough and was one of the hardest things for me to learn throughout my career. Slowly over the years I began to understand more and more about how important it was to stay humble and understand that everyone can make mistakes. You don't turn your back on them because they made a mistake, but learn from them so the next night you do things better.

Lessons learned in combat, and sometimes in blood, must be passed on.

CHAPTER 8

Shoot, Move, and Communicate

Relationships

The dogs were keeping up a steady bark as we patrolled toward the compound.

I could hear them as soon as the sound of the helicopter's engines faded. The first bark echoed through the valley as the team took our ritualistic piss after getting off our long helicopter ride. Seconds later, I heard a second one. By the time we were in patrol formation and started moving toward the target, it sounded like a choir of dogs alerting every farmer and fighter in the area to our presence.

I was now a veteran of eleven years in the SEALs and had been around long enough to become a team leader, and I was pretty well versed in the basic building blocks of operations. I no longer let standard human fears get in the way of making good decisions, and I knew communication and teamwork were the keys to success in combat.

That didn't mean anything came easy.

We had flown up to Kunduz, in northern Afghanistan. The Germans and other Coalition forces had been in charge of the northern part of Afghanistan for years at this point. They conducted very few, if any, offensive operations in the area. They were focused much more on building roads, schools, and clinics. With no one chasing them out, enemy fighters had begun using the area as a safe haven. Hell, I wouldn't want to leave the wire either, with a beer garden and several bars and clubs on base, but that was a different story.

We'd come up to northern Afghanistan after our intelligence analysts picked up a tip that a high-level Taliban commander was in the area. As the analysts continued the surveillance, we flew up to the area. We wanted to be close so we could launch once the operation got the green light.

We had no idea what the commander looked like, so the image of him on the briefing slide was just a silhouette.

Throughout the day, our analysts tracked the commander and watched via ISR as he moved from location to location, picking up fighters along the way. Finally, after the sun set, we observed the group move to what we call a bed-down location, usually a tree line or some defensible position where they would stop moving for the night and get some rest. It just so happened that the tree line they picked butted up against a large compound. It was standard practice for fighters to show up at a random civilian compound, demand to be fed, then, with full stomachs, fade into the tree line to sleep. With the thick vegetation of northern Afghanistan, it was easy for the fighters to simply patrol into the trees and hide from our drones flying overhead.

When the fighters arrived that afternoon, the drone pilots watched them go into the compound and then a few hours later disappear into the trees. From what we could see via ISR, the fighters never left the tree line. This didn't mean they hadn't moved through the trees and left the area. They were smart enough to know we had drones watching for them. The enemy would routinely move to multiple bed-down locations during the night.

In this case, the analysts were confident that the fighters hadn't moved from the tree line, so we decided to launch on the mission.

Since I was a team leader, I had the internal radio net in one ear that allowed me to talk to my teammates and the command net in the other ear that allowed me to talk with the troop commander, troop chief, and any drones or aviation assets patrolling above.

"No movement," the drone pilot said. "All the pax"— "pax" is shorthand for "people"—"are still in the tree line. It appears that the white station wagon is still in the same place."

The Taliban commander and his group of fighters used the car and several dirt bikes to move between villages. If the car was still parked in the same location near the compound, we were confident the fighters weren't far away.

The dogs barked for the entire seven-kilometer patrol. We were doing our best to be sneaky, and our snipers picked the best route in order to avoid the local villages. But after each step all I heard were the dogs. It definitely gave us all an uneasy feeling.

"These fucking dogs are killing me," Steve said as we took a short break. "Do they always bark this much, or do they work for the Taliban?"

Steve was a fellow team leader and one of my best friends in the command. He was "country" strong, with a thick chest and arms. He had a bushy beard that covered his face. It made him look like a groundhog. We joked about it so much it became his nickname.

I met the Groundhog during S&T. From the first day, when asked to rate the top five and bottom five in the class, I always put Steve in my top five, and he always stood out as a leader in the class. I was lucky to get assigned to the same squadron as he did. We were assigned to different teams, but we basically grew up together in the command. He was on all of my deployments and training trips. Steve was the guy I went to when I had an idea and wanted some feedback. We almost always saw eye to eye, so when he would tell me he didn't agree with something I was doing or had some advice for me, I always listened. His early advice was always the same.

"Take a wrap off, man," he would tell me. "If you're too emotional, no one is going to listen."

But Steve was also a lot like me.

He and I almost got sent home from a deployment after we were critical of the tactics of one of our troop chiefs. The troop chief hadn't asked for any guidance or input from any of the team leaders. He came up with a plan and refused to listen to the other leaders in the unit. The troop chief overheard us criticizing the plan. We were new to the command at this point and the troop chief didn't take kindly to us "new guys" questioning his plan. He threatened to send us home from deployment, but our team leaders protected us.

We worked together for six years before both of us got our own team in the same troop. As team leaders, we worked in concert. I knew his moves and he knew mine. We'd been teammates so long that when the shooting started I always knew how he was reading a situation and how he and his team would react.

The SEAL community has a saying that each team member has to be able to "shoot, move, and communicate." Being able to shoot means having the tactical skills needed to fire your gun safely and effectively. Moving refers to how you work as a team and how effectively and tactically you move around the battlefield. Communicating is all about speaking clearly and effectively so your teammates know what you're doing. After years working so closely together, we could move and react almost seamlessly in a combat situation. We looked for SEALs who not only mastered those skills, but fit into our team. I never worried about guys on target. They knew what to do when the bullets started flying. My biggest leadership challenge was mentoring and teaching them what to do back in the team room.

I've sat in on the review board screening candidates for S&T. The oral interview process came after the physical fitness test—which I'd almost failed when I screened—and is probably the most nerve-wracking part of screening for S&T. It doesn't take a lot of mental aptitude to run fast and do push-ups. That is more about will and preparation.

Most of the questions during the board were what-if scenarios that tested your integrity. The key was to have a reason for your actions and be able to logically explain the choice you made. One of the best questions was about range time. I was asked the question when I screened for S&T and in turn asked the question when it was my turn to sit as a member of the board.

"You're not getting the range time you think you need to adequately prepare for a deployment," the board would ask. "You want to do more shooting. Do you take some nine-millimeter rounds from work and go to the civilian range?"

I still remember my answer.

"Yes, absolutely," I immediately blurted out, sitting in my dress uniform, a fresh shave and haircut, trying not to look nervous.

"Wouldn't that be illegal?" one of the master chiefs on the board said.

"I'm not stealing them," I said. "I am shooting the ammo. The logistics of my team make it difficult to train. I can't check out my work gun and go to a work range because the closest range was at Camp Pendleton. It is over an hour drive away from where I work and is hardly ever available. Shooting those rounds is going to make me better at my job; besides, I would make sure to tell the guys that manage our ammo what I'm doing with them."

Apparently that was the right answer. At the time, I wasn't sure why. But after being in the command, I understood. It showed drive and initiative to go beyond the minimum training goals, both key ingredients for an S&T candidate. It was also a good example of how I would overcome an obstacle to better my skills and be an asset to the team. We wanted to see intrinsically motivated candidates who would go above and beyond to get the job done.

When I was on the board, I tried to get to know each candidate with an eye toward determining if he fit into the command's culture because there was a chance one day he might be on my team.

"What do you bring to the table? Why should we select you to attend S&T?" I always asked during the interview.

The top answer was always "I'm a really hard worker," followed by "I'm really good at CQB," or close quarters battle, meaning they were good at clearing rooms.

"So fucking what?" was my response. Everybody in the command was a hard worker and good at CQB. I wanted the guys who exceed the minimums. The basics of the job are a given. I wanted the guy who asked himself every day the same question:

How do I become an asset to the team?

We wanted guys who were always pushing, the ones who did something more than the basic job description. Everyone in our organization did what was asked of them, but we wanted the SEALs who did what was asked and then went out and found more work to do. That was being an asset to the team.

Like everything in the SEALs, the only way to succeed was being all in, all the time. Unlike other units that select operators from throughout the service, candidates selected for S&T come only from the SEAL teams. Our similar backgrounds and the fact that every operator had to complete the exact same standards to get into the unit made our command a very close-knit place to work. These relationships are very important not only to morale and a good working environment, but in combat as well. Our close-knit teams allowed us to anticipate each other's moves, which over time proved to be the difference between success and failure on target.

The dogs were still barking when we stopped at the edge of a big, muddy field opposite the compound and the tree line. I wished the dogs would shut up. Then again, I figured maybe the dogs always barked this much. Hopefully the enemy was deaf to them at this point.

We had a squad of Army Rangers and some Afghan commandos with us. They carried an assortment of weapons but for tonight's mission had carried several of the larger and heavier MK 48 machine guns. The MK 48 fired a 7.62-caliber bullet and could be very effective providing covering fire into thick tree lines and foliage. We waited as the Rangers along with our Afghan commando unit slowly crept through the waist-deep grass of the field and settled into an overwatch or support-by-fire position. If we got into some shit, we would be able to call them up to provide suppressive fire with the big guns. Once they were set, our troop flanked to the far-right side of the open field and along the edge of the tree line toward the enemy position.

The field was muddy and it took us a while to slowly move around to the tree line. Irrigation ditches ran along the outside of the trees, creating a barrier. If we could get the jump on whoever was in the tree line, they'd be trapped between the ditch and us. I could hear the Ranger platoon commander on the radio as his men watched for fighters. They hadn't spotted any movement, so we slowly entered the trees.

My team was in the middle. Steve's team was ahead of me. It was pitch-black. Even with night vision, it was hard to navigate the tight path through the trees because the branches blocked any ambient light. Everyone walked carefully, trying hard not to make any noise.

We all knew that one false step could alert the fighters hiding nearby. I was practically walking on my tippy toes in an attempt to be light on my feet. I could see friendly infrared lasers slowly scanning the area ahead. Each operator had a laser on his gun. The IR flood acted like a flashlight and the small IR dot in the middle of that spotlight was where your bullets would hit. They were invisible to the naked eye, but those of us wearing night vision goggles could see the lasers. The lasers helped us see, especially in the thick tree line.

Less than fifty yards into the trees and off to my right side, I saw Walt tense up and freeze. I'd worked with Walt long enough to know by his body language that he had spotted something. He didn't need to say a word. We all knew he had something in his sights.

Our entire force stopped in its tracks as Walt and another SEAL inched their way forward. I could see Walt wave us on as he continued to train his gun at the base of a large tree. As we got closer and moved past his position, I could see two fighters sound asleep on the ground. Their AK-47s were lying nearby. Trash was strewn all around the clearing. There were water bottles, cans of food, and bits of paper. Walt took a few steps deeper into the woods, his weapon at the ready. I saw his laser sight shining on the fighter's chest. He and another SEAL stayed put and covered the sleeping Taliban. Even though we were all using suppressed weapons, Walt made the right call and just sat there watching them sleep, waiting to react if and when they woke up. He didn't want to risk firing on them and making any noise that would wake up the rest of the Taliban.

Encountering the sleeping Taliban was both good news and bad news.

Good because the bad guys were definitely in the vicinity and hadn't moved out of the area. But it was bad because we were walking into a firefight. We continued to move silently, careful not to wake the sleeping fighters. About thirty yards past the camp, I saw the driveway that led up to the compound where they had eaten dinner. There were the motorcycles and the white station wagon parked under a giant tree in front of the house.

Moving up the driveway, my team was mixed in with Steve's team, minus Walt and another SEAL back with the Taliban sentries. There were five of us moving directly up the driveway toward the house. I glanced to the left and could read Steve's body language. He was thinking the same thing I was. We were about to come face-to-face with the enemy. Steve was crouched down, with his HK416 shouldered and ready to fire. His IR laser scanned the dark trees directly ahead of me.

Steve and his machine gunner, armed with an MK 46 light machine gun, flanked to the left of my group as we began making our way up the driveway. My team kept walking toward the compound and the clump of tangled trees behind it. We knew the fighters didn't have enough time to go far, nor would they venture out into the open for fear of being spotted by our drones. If they ran into the open, the Rangers set up on the edge of the field would spot them. If we were going to come into contact with the enemy, it would take place inside the tree line directly in front of us.

Near the top of the driveway, I saw a cluster of blankets and mats on the ground. The blankets were in a pile and looked like whoever was under them had gotten up quickly. There were multiple sleeping mats, at least five that I could see on my first glance. I didn't bother to count because my mind was fixed on the coming fight.

"OK, shit, where are they?" I thought.

As soon as I spotted the mats, I stopped and began pointing them out to my team using my IR laser. Everyone froze as we started to scan the surrounding wood line. I could see my teammates' IR lasers crisscrossing over the trees. I slowly tracked my laser across the dark tree line to our left when a head popped up in front of me and then disappeared. It was too fast to positively identify if it was a man, woman, or child.

With the rules of engagement constantly changing and becoming more restrictive, I couldn't shoot because I had no idea if what I'd seen was a fighter. The odds were definitely good that the head belonged to someone from the nearby bedrolls. If so, based on the sentries Walt had picked out, I was pretty sure he would be armed, but I couldn't see a gun and we hadn't been fired upon. Everything was right in front of me. These had to be bad guys. I'd already seen the car, motorcycles, and empty bedrolls and was pretty damn sure this was one of the guys we were looking for.

Without seeing any more activity, I keyed up my radio.

"Hey, guys, I've got some movement over here," I whispered into the radio.

Just as I finished the radio call, a now very obvious enemy fighter stood up out of the ditch fifteen yards directly in front of us. As he stood up he began firing from a belt-fed PKM machine gun.

The muzzle flash looked like he was shooting a howitzer. A three-foot-long flame shot from the barrel as I fell backward and landed on my back. Everything in my night vision goggles exploded in a burst of light. Rounds tore overhead as the gunman fired wildly. The roar of the gun drowned out everything, including any thoughts I had about rules of engagement or what to do. I could see several of my teammates diving for cover. My body switched to survival mode. I had just pulled some *Matrix*-style bullet dodging and fallen backward onto my back. If I dove forward I'd land in the path of the bullets chewing up the ground around me. I just wanted to get as low as I possibly could, as fast as I possibly could. We were completely pinned down, with zero cover. It would be only a matter of seconds until the rounds from the PKM began tearing my team apart.

I jammed my rifle between my legs and started shooting back toward the enemy. I could feel the spent cartridges hit against my thigh. I wasn't aiming through my EOTech and couldn't see where my IR laser was pointed. Front sight focus was out the window as I fired rounds at the target by feel alone. This time, I was spraying and praying. My teammates were also firing back. We needed to get some rounds back toward the fighter as quickly as possible.

Machine gun rounds slammed into the ground around us. Tracers buzzed by my face, slamming into trees and shrubs all around my team. Had any one of us stood up, we would have immediately been shot. The Taliban fighter was having trouble aiming the machine gun as it kicked up and down in his arms. But with each passing second, he was wrestling it under control.

All of a sudden I began hearing something a short distance to my left. It was the sweet sound of an MK46 machine gun. We typically shoot six- to eight-round bursts to conserve ammo and to help control the accuracy. But these weren't short bursts. Steve's gunner wasn't letting up on the trigger. He let fly one super-long continuous burst. He and Steve were about ten yards to our left and had a perfect angle on the enemy position. I could see his tracer rounds sending bits of wood and bark flying into the air as he walked the rounds directly on top of the enemy position.

The enemy fire completely died at this point, but the Squad Automatic Weapon (SAW) gunner and Steve were still providing covering fire. My team peeled back away from the PKM.

"Go," I yelled to a pair of my teammates while I continued to fire. Another member of my team stayed to help me cover the first pair.

After the first teammates bounded back a short distance, they found a safer position. It was my turn to move. I rolled onto my side and jumped up, careful to stay as low as I could. I was sure it would be only a moment before the PKM began firing again. This was our one chance to get out of the direct line of fire. Sprinting down the driveway, I slid to a stop just past my teammates. I leveled my rifle and started to fire in an attempt to provide covering fire for my teammates.

"Set," I yelled. "Go, go."

With all my guys back at the edge of the field and behind cover, we turned and provided as much covering fire as we could so Steve and his gunner could sprint to safety. The gunner had emptied an entire two-hundred-round box in one pull of the trigger. As he and Steve ran past me, I could see the gunner reloading his machine gun while in a dead sprint.

Once Steve and the gunner made it back, the troop chief cleared the Ranger platoon hot. They opened fire with heavy machine guns, grenade launchers, and small arms. It was impossible to hear anything over the roar of the guns. The Rangers were laying down a wall of bullets. I took a quick glance back toward where we had just been and saw trees exploding into kindling.

The troop chief and troop commander were huddled nearby working the radios.

"Get head counts and let me know we're all up," the troop commander said.

It was the team leaders' responsibility to make sure we all had one hundred percent accountability of all our guys. We certainly weren't going to leave anybody behind. I walked back to the line where my team had set up.

"Hell yeah," said one of my teammates.

I could just make out a smirk under his night vision goggles.

"Yeah, dude, what the fuck?" I said.

I don't think I could form a complete intelligent sentence if I wanted to. I had other things on my mind and knew I needed to get a head count before our JTAC could start dropping bombs. If we'd left a guy wounded back in the line of fire, we weren't going to be able to call in air support until we went back and got him. Luckily, everyone had made it back to the line.

I keyed my radio.

"Alpha is up," I said.

"Charlie is up," Steve said over the radio.

I held my breath as each team checked in over the radio

with their status. In my mind there was no way in hell everyone got away uninjured. The fighters had gotten the first rounds off at us. They had a head start and with the PKM firing six hundred and fifty to seven hundred and fifty rounds a minute, someone must have been hit.

All the reports came in clean. No one was injured. We didn't have to be good all the time. Sometimes it was better to be lucky. And so far our luck was holding.

Steve and his gunner had saved our lives. We all saw the same situation unfolding and he knew where my team was going to be and put his team in place to support us. If it weren't for Steve's team and the close bond we shared, there is no doubt we would have taken casualties. He instinctively knew what to do based off the terrain and our immediate reaction to the enemy fire. We thought the same way. We knew each other's position without thinking about it.

Think of a pickup basketball game out on the playground, but imagine that game being played by NBA players. No one is on the sideline diagramming plays with a chalkboard. They are individually great athletes and they can read off of each other to make amazing plays. We were doing the same thing, just not on the court and certainly not for the same paychecks.

"Stand by for CAS," I heard over the radio.

The JTAC was on the radio calling in Close Air Support. Fighters overhead started to circle, preparing for a bombing run.

"Three minutes," the troop chief said.

If there were any fighters left in the trees, they had three minutes to clear out before the bombs started to fall. I made sure my team had cover and waited for the strikes.

I hunkered down in a small ditch and waited for the whistling noise the bomb makes just before it detonates. Then I saw the bright flash lighting up the sky seconds before the thunderous crack of the explosion. I could make out the trees and compound in silhouette against the explosion as dirt and debris landed on us.

"Cleared hot for immediate re-attack," I heard over the radio. "Three minutes out."

The impact of the bombs in the tree line definitely made me happy that I wasn't on the receiving end. As each bomb impacted the ground and exploded, I could feel the shock wave thumping the terrain. It felt like a giant smashing his fists into the ground.

After the second bombing run, I met with the troop commander, troop chief, and other team leaders.

"We're going to clear out the tree line," the troop chief said. "Let me know when your teams are ready to roll."

A mix of guys from my team and Steve's team got up out of the ditch and prepared to move back up the driveway. We set up on a line and cautiously patrolled back into the tree line. As I got closer, the tree line looked like how I imagine a World War I battlefield would look. Craters where bombs had landed still smoldered. Charred trees shorn in half stood like broken teeth. A layer of smoke hung over everything. All of the trees were burning, creating a blinding green blur in our night vision goggles and making it almost impossible to see anything clearly.

Halfway up the driveway, I could see the area where we had taken the initial contact. It didn't look anything like it had looked a few minutes prior. The bombs had chewed up the thicket of trees, leaving just a smoking hole. Up ahead, I could make out the silhouette of something life-size lying in a small ditch. I held my rifle on the object as I approached. Moving closer, I saw it was one of the fighters. His body was badly burned. His clothes were still smoldering. I could see where shrapnel had cut through his long, baggy shirt. A chest rack hung from his torso. Another badly burned body was lying nearby.

We continued clearing through the burned-up tree line, stepping over pieces of debris and moving around the large craters left by the blast. I was about to pull my team back and start searching the compound and camp for any additional fighters or intelligence when the drone pilots circling above came over the radio.

"We have multiple movers one hundred and fifty meters to the west," the pilot said.

Six fighters had popped out of the tree line after the last bombing run. They must have been the luckiest six Taliban in the world. They somehow survived our initial firefight, the Rangers' heavy-weapons barrage, and now two bombing runs.

As the radio call came through, I looked over and saw Steve and his team to my left. We were both thinking the same thing. There was no way these guys were going to get away.

"Alpha Team has it," I said over the radio to the troop chief. Immediately following me on the radio Steve chimed in.

"Charlie Team has it."

Our troop chief paused for a second.

"Roger that," he said. "Alpha and Charlie, take control of ISR and the AC-130 gunship and let me know if you need anything else."

I checked in with the drone over the radio.

"ISR, this is Alpha One," I said. "I have an element of eight and one dog moving west at this time. Please advise with enemy numbers and position."

The drone pilot got us oriented and we quickly moved our two teams into position and started to patrol toward the enemy location. The dog handler pushed his combat dog out front. I could see it searching the ground for a scent. On the radio, we were getting reports from the ISR.

"Alpha One this is ISR," the drone pilot said. "We have multiple movers that are located at the southwest corner of an open field roughly five hundred meters to your west."

"Roger, ISR, please sparkle," I said.

The drone's sensor operator fired an infrared laser, like a giant laser pointer, at the fighters' location. Under our night vision, it looked like a giant finger pointing to the fighters' exact location. It was something out of a video game.

Once we broke out of the trees, we slowed way down. The tree line opened into a large field with a small levee and a thicket of trees running along the south end.

I watched our dog handler let his dog off the leash and push him ahead of the group along the edge of the trees. Steve's team moved on a line perpendicular to the trees. I noticed Steve's team was again taking a wide arc to my left, covering our flank.

I pushed my team farther to the right, hoping to get a better angle on the fighters. We didn't have the Rangers with us. It was up to the two assault teams. If we got into contact now, we would have two teams in position to open fire.

I stayed focused on the "sparkle." It hadn't moved since we cleared the tree line, which was good. But I wanted to close with the fighters before they could set up a defense. My hope was the fighters were trying to hide and not fight.

I checked to my left and right. My team was spread out and silently moving across the field. I glanced to my left over toward Steve's team and happened to notice our dog—nicknamed the hair missile—dive into the thicket of trees. The dog disappeared and then I heard a man let out a scream. The dog had locked onto the scent of a fighter and now I could hear its snarls and the man's screams.

My team kept an eye on the group of enemy fighters up ahead. Steve and one of the snipers moved into the tree line to help the dog. We could hear the man yelling as the dog tore into him. The yelling stopped after a few quick shots from the sniper's suppressed HK416.

Steve came over the radio.

"Fellas, watch your step. We just stumbled across a fighter hiding in the ditch with an RPG and ready to fire," he said.

The group of fighters we were chasing had dropped this guy off to ambush us as we passed. The dog found him and likely saved our lives in the process. These fighters weren't rookies. They weren't running scared but instead attempting to set up on us.

"ISR, Alpha One," I said. "Any movement from our group of fighters?"

"Alpha One, ISR," the pilot said. "Negative. They are still in place and my sparkle is on."

I saw Steve's team get back on line and begin moving forward along the edge of the trees. I didn't even need a radio call from Steve to know what he was thinking; I could simply tell from his body language. I responded by pushing my team farther out to the right flank to get a better flanking position. We were set up in a perfect "L" formation and would be able to hit the group of Taliban from both sides. The drone kept sparkling the fighters' location. It was dark and there was no way they could see us.

Step-by-step we closed to one hundred and fifty yards. Our lasers now joined the drone's.

They didn't have a chance.

With a massive IR floodlight from the ISR drone, the figures were easily identifiable in our night vision goggles. All five fighters had settled into a small perimeter and were lying there on the lip of a ditch waiting for us to approach.

They didn't know it yet, but it was too late for them. They couldn't see us but we could see them. The first shots killed two. I saw them drop like they'd been pulled into the ground by a cable. I could see our lasers dance around them as fighter after fighter crumpled and disappeared into the ditch. One fighter opened up with his AK-47, spraying our direction, but the rounds sailed well over our heads. The shooter went down in a heap after several rounds slammed into him.

The fight took only a few seconds and the outcome was never in doubt. We moved forward and searched all the enemy bodies, collecting all the weapons and blowing them in place. While we cleared the bodies and weapons, the rest of the SEALs and Rangers secured the initial target.

Once we were done, we patrolled back to the compound and then back to the helicopters.

Nothing we do is rocket science, but being able to work as a team is taught to us throughout our SEAL careers, and a key ingredient in our success. It was like a pickup basketball game, except we were focused on shooting, moving, and communicating.

There is no secret sauce. Every SEAL has gone through the same training, tested themselves in the same kind of extreme conditions, and typically trained together extensively to the point where we all wind up capable of doing the most basic tasks extraordinarily well. That gives us unshakeable confidence in each other. The relationship Steve and I had developed over years of working together meant we could handle almost any situation, and our trust is what allowed us to succeed even when the fight didn't go as we planned. The importance we put on those close-knit relationships was the factor that most often tipped the needle from defeat to victory.

CHAPTER 9

Follow Your Buddy

Accountability

It was the night before the operation was going to launch when I got the call to come over to the joint operations center. It was 2007 and I was on my sixth deployment. Instead of working with my team and doing raids, I had been sent to work with other government agencies as a liaison.

I'd coordinate air support and help with the tactical plan. I'd also take responsibility for any prisoners that we would detain so they could be turned over to the appropriate Coalition military detention facility.

The relationships between the CIA, Special Forces, and the 82nd Airborne Division nearby were strained at best. The Special Forces team wanted to go out and patrol but didn't have the money to pay the Afghan police unit they were training. In order to set up an ambush along a trail used by fighters to come across the border, we had to send up a CONOP, or concept of operations plan, indicating we were going out to train on "ambushes," in order to get it approved.

At this point in the war, bureaucracy was slowing everything down. In order to get outside the wire, we'd first put together several PowerPoint slides explaining the operation.

The slides would have to be approved all the way up the chain of command, which could take several days.

A little over halfway into our deployment, I got a call from my squadron to report to a base in eastern Afghanistan. The message was loud and clear.

It was almost unheard of for them to call us in from our assignment. The rest of my squadron was spread all over Afghanistan doing the same mission. When word came to come back for a mission, I wasn't upset. I enjoyed my mission, but I also liked the idea of getting back to being an assaulter with the rest of the team.

Once our squadron was reconstituted, we met in the main planning room. The briefs were held in a long, narrow room with handmade wooden benches running down the middle, like a church. At the front of the room were flat-screen TVs for PowerPoint presentations and to show us drone video or satellite photos. Maps of Afghanistan and the border area hung on one wall opposite wire diagrams showing key players in the various Taliban and al Qaeda networks we were targeting.

The room was packed full of people. It was standing room only. Up front, the squadron commander started the brief. A source had reported that he had seen Osama bin Laden, the al Qaeda leader, near Tora Bora. It was the same place U.S. forces almost captured him in 2001.

The Battle of Tora Bora started December 12, 2001, and lasted five days. It was believed Bin Laden was hiding in the mountains at Tora Bora, which is Pashto for "black cave." He was suspected of being in a cave complex in the White Mountains, near the Khyber Pass. His headquarters was rumored to be a multistory complex equipped with hydroelectric power from mountain streams, hotel-like corridors, and room for a thousand fighters. The cave complex was definitely a historical safe haven for Afghan fighters, and the CIA had funded many of the improvements to the region during the 1980s to assist the mujahedeen during the Soviet invasion of Afghanistan.

Troops during the battle in 2001 found massive weapons caches with Stinger missiles from the 1980s. U.S. and Afghan forces overran the Taliban and al Qaeda positions but failed to kill or capture Bin Laden at that time. He escaped to Pakistan. Now a CIA source said he was coming back to Afghanistan.

"They saw a tall man in flowing white robes in Tora Bora," the commander said. "He was back to possibly make his final stand."

I wasn't that excited.

Something wasn't right. The operation was based on a single human source that claimed to see a tall man in "flowing white robes." Single-source intelligence rarely ended up being accurate and typically wasn't enough on its own to convince us to launch on an operation.

With no other sources to confirm the report, we launched dozens of ISR drones into the area. They flew missions day and night over Tora Bora with no significant sightings. It's funny because the intelligence folks and higher-level planners always seem to think that you can't hear drones. The reality is you can. The drones fly in the middle of the mountains in Afghanistan and sound like a lawn mower circling above. In Afghanistan, that sound can mean only one thing, an American drone. Send in a couple dozen of them and anyone in the area is going to know someone is watching.

The mission was set to launch in a few days, but we were ready to go on the first night. We'd been at this for long enough that we didn't need much notice. We were quick thinkers, and it didn't require a long lead time to plan and execute a mission. But being ready quickly didn't really matter because the operation kept getting delayed.

Day after day it was a new excuse.

"We're waiting on B-1 bombers."

"The Rangers aren't in place yet."

"We've got Special Forces heading to the area with their Afghan units."

The delays were coming from higher up. It seemed every general in Afghanistan wanted to be involved. Units from every service had been read in. Even the Army's M142 High Mobility Artillery Rocket System, which was built to shoot long-range missiles, got a part of the mission. It was on tap to shoot a barrage of rockets into the area to provide pre-assault fires a short time before the SEALs would fly in by helicopter.

With each delay, what we call the "good-idea fairy" gained momentum. Officers and planners started dreaming up crazy scenarios for us to deal with on the mission, and somehow it always meant more equipment to carry.

Besides the extra units, the FBI sent their DNA experts all

the way from Washington. Someone had also spent thirty thousand dollars on a 3-D map of the valley. It showed up one day, only to sit in the back of the briefing room, unused. The only time we looked at it was to see exactly what a thirty-thousand-dollar map looked like.

After a few days of waiting, I was hanging out by the fire pit in the center of our camp. We were sitting around talking about all the madness that was transpiring around us when a buddy of mine walked up.

"Hey, man, has master chief tracked you down?" he said.

"Nope," I replied. "What's up?"

"Not sure, but I guess you aren't going on the mission anymore and are being tasked to do something a bit different."

My curiosity was up. I walked over to the operations center. As I walked inside the ops center there was a nonstop bustle of activity. There must have been twelve flat-screen TVs on the wall, all looking at a different area. I saw my master chief at his seat in the corner and made my way over to him.

"What you got, brother?" I said. "I hear you're looking for me."

"Something came up, and you and Walt are going to work with some folks and possibly help them conduct some targets," the master chief said. "We got you a plane tonight. From there you'll link up with your contact and make your way up to the border region near Tora Bora. We need you guys to coordinate blocking positions. If we get squirters, you guys can make sure he doesn't get away again."

"Am I bringing my kit?" I asked.

"Yeah," he said. "Bring all your op gear.

"Since both you and Walt are JTACs you can help coordinate any air strikes as well as passing intel from the ISR to the
soldiers on the ground."

Walt was going to be my swim buddy, a technique taught to
us at BUD/S. SEALs never go anywhere alone. From the first
day on the beach during BUD/S, we are paired with a swim
buddy. The Army uses the same principle, but they call them
"battle buddies." On missions overseas or training missions
back in the States, your swim buddy always watches your back.

But the idea of having a swim buddy means a lot more
than that. They have your best interests at heart and are not
afraid to tell you the truth. Your swim buddy isn't your boss
or a subordinate. He is your peer. Swim buddies check your
parachute, listen to your plans, and are usually the first people
to tell you, "Fuck no, that's stupid."

Succeeding is much easier when you have someone else
holding you accountable. Having swim buddies is a two-way
street. Not only do you need to be honest and communicate;
you have to listen. Otherwise, the message is lost. I learned
over my career that my swim buddy was even more valuable
as we negotiated the politics of the command. I needed a peer
who would call me out.

Steve, Walt's team leader, was my swim buddy for most of
my career. We were in S&T together and grew up in the same
squadron. We could speak honestly, and when he told me I was
fucking up or getting too emotional about an issue, I listened.

You always want someone in your professional life who is

going to be honest, who's going to call you on your bull-shit. But a swim buddy is a guy who not only will call you on your bullshit but will also without a doubt have your back when things get rough. They don't disown you when you make a mistake. They don't ever walk away from you when you need help. They are friends, mentors, and your last sanity check. You can trust them implicitly, and like in BUD/S, they are never that far away from you when the bullets start flying.

██████████████████████████████████████

███████████████████████

██████████████████████████████████████

████

██████████████████████████████

███████████████████████

██████████████████████████████████████

██████████████████████████████████████

██████████████████████████████

█████████████

██████████████████████████████████████

███████████████████████

██████████████████████████████████████

██████████████████████████████████

██████████████████████████████████████

███████████████████████

██████████████████████████████████████

██████████████████████████████████████

██████████████████████████████████████

████████████

██████████████████████████████████████

█████████████████████████

████████████

Walt was going to be my swim buddy.

I raced back to my room and got my stuff packed. The base was built to house about two hundred people, but in a week the population had grown to almost seven hundred. The chow hall was jammed every meal. There was no room. Hot showers became a commodity. At first, there was never any hot water; then there was no water at all. Then the toilets got stopped up.

At night, we'd sit around the campfire at the center of our compound and laugh about how massive the mission had become. The operation alone was going to begin as a massive bombing campaign. More bombs were going to be dropped in Tora Bora than had been dropped in all of Afghanistan from the beginning of the war.

"We could have been in and out of there already," Walt told me one night. "All this commotion is only going to give away what we're planning. Shit, I'll be surprised if anybody is still in that mountain range. Lord knows if I heard drones flying above my house for the past week, I'd leave town."

All the commotion at our compound also attracted the attention of the Afghans who worked at the camp. It's kind of hard to keep anything a secret when you have no less than fifty local Afghans working on your compound, pumping the shitters, filling the water barrels, and doing construction. There was no doubt in any of our minds that everybody knew who we were and that we were spinning up on something big.

Plus, every day the mission was delayed, there was a better chance of it leaking. As we sat at the flight line waiting for our plane, Walt and I both had the same feeling about the mission. Our money was on a dry hole.

"Here is what is going to happen," I said finally. "They'll

land and spend a week hiking around the mountains. It's a multimillion-dollar camping trip."

Walt agreed.

"Sucks to be them," he said. "At least our trip will be an adventure."

We were headed to another Central Asian country. On the way, we spent a night in the capital and then moved back toward the border. But at our first stop, the host country said Walt had to stay behind. They were going to allow only one of us to link up with their forces stationed along the border. Since I was senior in rank, it fell to me. I didn't much like the idea of heading over the border without my swim buddy, but I didn't have a choice.

After spending another night in Peshawar, I headed out to the airport to catch a helicopter to a base across the border with Tora Bora. Instead of Walt, a CIA officer called Harvey and a communications tech from the unit now joined me. I met Harvey at the embassy. He was tall and thin and still kept his hair short in a Marine Corps flattop.

A former artillery officer, he was sporting the CIA's "go to war" uniform of 5.11 Tactical pants, a North Face polo shirt, and hiking boots. I'd worked with the agency before and I wanted to feel this guy out a little bit. We'd be "swim buddies" for the next week or so, but I wasn't sure he understood the concept like I did.

"So, man, what is your tasking?" I asked.

Harvey shrugged.

"Been up to this area before?" I asked.

"Nope," he said. "I've been at the embassy for a while, but this is the first time in this part of the country."

"Great," I thought, "another one fresh off the cocktail circuit." This was the first time he would be this close to the actual war. Since I worked at the outstation, I'd spent a lot of time with the agency. They all seemed to have advanced degrees, but no common sense when it came to Afghanistan. They spent more time fighting each other. The agency, in my experience, was one big pissing contest.

At the airport we sat on the tarmac and waited for our helicopter to show up. Keeping tight schedules and being on time was something the host country was definitely not used to.

After several hours of sitting around, we were met by a gaggle of officers who ushered us into the most rundown Mi-17 cargo helicopter I'd ever seen. Built by the Russians, the Mi-17 didn't have the sleek look of American helicopters. Instead, it looked like a fat insect with a bulbous body and a tail boom jutting out. Paint was peeling off the side, and the cabin deck was slick in places from oil or some other fluid. I found a spot on the floor near the back and hoped for the best.

Harvey climbed in next to me, followed by the communications tech.

The helicopter slowly came to life as we lifted off and climbed into the sky. I tried to relax and not focus on the hydraulic fluid leaking from the ceiling as we flew. Something else was wrong as well. The whole helicopter seemed to be tilted to the left. We weren't even balanced correctly.

The crew chief started to move boxes of meals ready to eat

and Pelican cases and gear bags back and forth, trying to balance the helicopter. No matter how hard he tried, it never leveled out. Between moving boxes, he started brewing tea in a small electric pot. The first two cups went to the pilots, delivered on a small silver tray. The second cups went to Harvey and me, again delivered on the same tray.

I sipped tea and tried not to think about crashing. Next to me, Harvey sat silently and looked out the window. It was hard to talk over the engine noise.

We landed at the base without incident. The officers were nervous once we arrived. When I tried to help unload the bags, the officers shooed me away and escorted me to a nearby truck. A captain greeted us. His skin was dark and weathered from the sun. A well-groomed mustache covered his lip.

He seemed nervous and agitated.

"It is better you stay in the truck," he said. "My men will bring your things up to your area."

The convoy snaked its way from the airfield up a rutted road toward a bunch of buildings. The base looked nothing like ours in Afghanistan. It was wide open, with no walls, and sat in the bottom of a bowl surrounded by mountains. We were located so close to Tora Bora that I could literally look at the mountains in the distance and see the bombs going off.

The trucks stopped at a building concealed behind a fence. It was still on the base, but far enough away where we couldn't be easily seen. While the communications tech set up all of the radios and computers, I found an empty room and started to unpack.

The U-shaped building was made of concrete. Most of the rooms were empty. We each had a room with a bunk bed, but no mattress, just a box spring on a wire frame. Harvey came into my room.

"They give you any sheets?" he asked, eyeballing my kit and rifle out on the bed.

"Nope," I said. "I'm just going to use my sleeping bag and the ground pad that I packed."

He looked annoyed and glanced back into the hallway and then back at me.

"You think they have sheets for us?"

A platoon of soldiers arrived to protect us. They lived in another house next door but kept soldiers posted on the roof and on roving patrols around our building twenty-four hours a day.

I didn't think they had sheets for him.

"Doubt it," I said. "But you can ask."

He left and returned about a half hour later. He had a set of sheets in his hands.

"They have sheets if you want some," he said. "They had to go around the base and find them. They're kind of rough."

There was no way I was going to ask for sheets. As Harvey's swim buddy, I probably should have squared him away, but I think I was taken aback by how inconsiderate he was acting. He seemed to think the soldiers were there to cater to us. We were the visitors and should have been content with whatever they gave us. I knew full well that we weren't going to be living in the Four Seasons. I packed accordingly and didn't plan on making a fuss. My new swim buddy was already coming across as the ugly American.

It quickly became clear that the mission was out of Harvey's comfort zone. This was not what he'd been trained to do. He seemed more interested in being comfortable and didn't seem too focused on the objective. My goal was to build a relationship with the soldiers so if and when we saw squirters attempting to escape the upcoming bombing campaign, I could leverage that relationship and hopefully they would allow me to go out on the operation with them.

That night, I joined the soldiers for dinner. We had a chicken stew with flatbread and several platters of fresh vegetables. We sat around a blanket, our shoes off, and ate with our hands. Some of the soldiers spoke English and we spent the dinner talking about the area and how years ago, it had been a beautiful vacation spot. It was now Taliban controlled and no longer safe.

Harvey was also invited to dinner, but declined and sat in his room eating an MRE. He showed up after dinner looking for some sugar for his coffee. The only sugar we had was raw, which he reluctantly stirred into his cup.

"I like granulated better. Can you get me some of that type of sugar?" he asked the officer in charge of our guards.

He wasn't making many friends, and by the third day, you could see how much the host country's officers disliked him. If he wasn't in the makeshift operations center, he was in his room. At night, he used to wear a pair of short running shorts that barely covered his groin and a tank top that exposed his slender, pasty white arms. It was amazing how bad he was at building rapport.

None of this was rocket science.

The Army Special Forces get extensive training in dealing with local nationals, but this was all new to me too. Then again, I think my growing up in an Alaskan Eskimo village had something to do with my own attitude. I was comfortable dealing with a foreign culture. It was no different than making friends in school or at work. Just be yourself, be open, and be a good houseguest.

For a guy who worked for an agency tasked with winning over sources and building rapport with the locals, Harvey didn't have a clue. At every turn, he offended our hosts. From the sheets to the sugar to the tank top, he damaged every bridge I tried to build.

Harvey was making it impossible for me to build rapport. Even though I had a good relationship with the soldiers, when Harvey walked into the room the mood changed. The soldiers became stiff and formal. Their body language gave away their disdain for him. He wasn't accountable at all for his actions. Harvey was thinking about only himself, and not the mission. And by doing that—having that mind-set, which is the antithesis of the SEAL philosophy—he jeopardized the success of the mission. In his community there was very little teamwork, which to me was alien because the team was the bedrock of the SEAL community. At this point in my career, I'd worked only on kick-ass teams. Shit, even when I worked with the Polish GROM during Operation Iraqi Freedom my first deployment, they fit in perfectly with our SEAL platoons. I assumed that everyone was like we were.

I also knew if my teammates forced any fighters across the border, there was no way they were going to allow me to tag along. At this point I wasn't even sure I'd want to go into the field with Harvey as my swim buddy. I missed Walt.

With the mission under way on the Afghan side of the border, I sat in our small command center and scanned all the ISR feeds. Based off the radio traffic and what I was seeing on my screens, nobody seemed to be moving in my direction. For that matter, nobody seemed to be moving in the Tora Bora region altogether.

My squadron assaulted onto the top of the deserted Tora Bora mountain range the day after I left. They set up at a patrol base. From there, they started to search the area. The FBI's DNA expert arrived on the third wave of helicopters and promptly got altitude sickness. She had to be medevaced out twelve hours later. So much for that good-idea fairy.

A couple of times during the mission, I'd have to call in the officers after one of the Predators saw a large group of men with guns moving along the border, only to be told the group was part of the host nation's forces. One time, the Predators spotted what looked like a camp near the border. I could make out tents and several men with guns walking around the area. They didn't appear to be in uniform, but after an investigation with our host, he reported that it was just a border checkpoint.

After several days with little to no activity and the operation starting to wind down, the PakMil sent word back to the embassy that they didn't want us there anymore. The next day, Harvey and I packed our gear and climbed aboard the same ratty MI-17 helicopter. Over a cup of tea, I watched the mountains slip by as the helicopter—still cockeyed—flew us back to the capital, where I met back up with Walt. We were both frustrated and ready to go back to some real work.

I told Walt what happened with Harvey. It dawned on both of us just how lucky we were to be in the unit where your swim buddy would take his shirt off his back for you. There was no AAR between Harvey and me, and no chance for us to discuss lessons learned. He wasn't interested in being a good teammate and I never felt like he had my back. I was happy that I'd never see him again

We boarded a plane to fly back to Afghanistan. Walt and I were flying back with a half dozen other diplomats and soldiers. Just as I settled into my seat, the door opened and the young State Department staffer who took us to the plane climbed back onboard.

He'd set up the flight, but now he looked pale and nervous. Right behind him were several customs officials with AK-47s. From what I could gather, they wanted to know who was on the plane and the State Department staffer didn't have any answers. The staffer was no older than twenty-five and probably hadn't been in the country more than a few months.

Walt and I had our guns, explosives, and all our operations gear in our bags. As ordered, we'd brought everything we'd need to go into the field.

"Leave all your stuff," the staffer said to everybody. "They told me the plane can leave, but only if you all get off. You all have to get off the plane right away."

I could see the stress on his face. The staffer kept looking back at the officials. Something was really wrong. I glanced over at the guards. They looked angry.

As the others got up to leave, Walt and I ditched our pistols by hiding them in our bags and followed the staffer. Outside on the tarmac, a guard shoved his rifle in my face and started to scream at the group. I held up my hands and smiled. It felt strange to be without my pistol. It wasn't like I was going to start fighting customs inspectors, but the weapon was a security blanket for me. I felt naked without it. I could see Walt sizing up the guards and assessing the situation. He was always the little guy with the big personality.

A few years before, I invited Walt out to SHOT Show, a shooting trade show in Las Vegas. We'd usually go out there to meet with vendors and see what kinds of new guns and gear were available on the market that we might be able to use.

The first day, I introduced him around to all the vendors. By the second day, my contacts were asking me where Walt was hanging out. At a bar after the show the third night, I found Walt holding court with executives from the National Rifle Association. He had a cigar in his mouth, and he was slapping backs and shaking hands like he was running for office.

But one look at the guards and I was sure his winning personality wasn't going to help here. We were in a lot of trouble. We weren't sure what was going on, but from the looks of it, we weren't going to talk our way out of this one.

We were herded into a waiting room near the flight line. Walt sat down in the chair next to me. I could just make out his exasperated grimace through his beard. He kept his head down and his eyes low.

"This is bullshit," he growled.

A couple of the diplomats and younger soldiers began showing signs of stress. They were beginning to get more and more upset. The State Department staffer who pulled us off the airplane wasn't in the room, so to me that was a good sign. Hopefully he was working out whatever issues there were. I looked over our group and could tell that there were some very worried folks.

"Hey, guys, everyone just needs to relax. I'm sure this is being worked out right this second," I said. "Let's just all keep our mouths shut and wait to hear more."

There were multiple guards armed with AK-47s standing in the room, and there was no doubt in my mind that they spoke English. They were not only guarding us, but also listening to everything we said, waiting for someone to slip up and say something they shouldn't.

We sat in the room for almost an hour. The guards kept coming in and demanding our military ID cards or passports. Once they made copies of those, I guess, they wanted our driver's licenses and any other documents we could produce.

Each time, I'd hold the document up, only to have it snatched out of my hand by the guard. He'd growl something at me in Urdu and march off. My mind was spinning. Why did they let the plane leave, but not us? What exactly were they looking for? Why were they harassing us? I started to wonder if I had diplomatic immunity.

Then the State Department staffer was back with the guards. No one looked happy, but the color had returned to the staffer's face. Instead of that frazzled look, he now just looked tired.

"OK, we can go," he said. "Head out to the van. They are going to let us go back to the embassy."

As we passed, the guard's scowl got more severe. Walt and I pulled the staffer aside in the van. We wanted to know what had happened as well as where our gear was. We never traveled without our weapons and kit, and it felt wrong to leave them behind.

"What's the deal?" Walt said.

"I finally got to my boss at the embassy and he made some calls," the staffer said. "The plane was allowed to leave, but your kit will have to meet you back in Afghanistan."

"OK, so our kit is safe. Now, what the fuck was up with that entire situation?" I asked angrily.

The staffer was flustered again. He stammered out something about a mix-up. I turned and looked at Walt and could already tell that he was thinking the whole explanation was suspect.

"My money is on the fact that you fucked up and forgot to file the proper paperwork," I said to the staffer.

He didn't respond, but kept talking about getting us home.

"I'm going to need to work some angles, so it may be a few days before I can get you guys out and back to Afghanistan," he said.

After lying low at the American Embassy for a few days, we were allowed to leave. Walt and I landed back in Afghanistan a week later and couldn't have been happier. We both had gotten a healthy dose of what it's like to work without a swim buddy, and neither one of us wanted to repeat it anytime soon. While I had endured living with a horrible version of a swim buddy, Walt had stayed at the American Embassy without one at all. He was left with no mission and no support. All he had to do was kill time. We were not only happy to be back and linked up together, but very appreciative of each other's support.

When all was said and done, the Air Force essentially knocked the tops off a few of the Tora Bora Mountains and my teammates went on a weeklong camping trip. There was no sign of any man in flowing white robes. My money is still on the fact that the single-source intelligence was shit from the beginning. We'd never forget the "flowing white robes," and from that point on, the term became slang for a mission that was all fucked up from the start.

I'd remember the mission for another reason too. Working without trust, solid communication, and the ability to pull your partner aside and give him or her your honest opinion—and get honest feedback in return—was tough for me. Good, bad, or otherwise, your swim buddy is there to protect you, encourage you, give advice, call you on your shit, and most importantly be there when you need help.

CHAPTER 10

Comfortable Being Uncomfortable

Discomfort

It was Alaska cold.

Not kind of cold.

Not partially cold or even the type of cold where you think you could go without gloves and a hat.

I'm talking bone chilling cold that hits you at your core.

I couldn't feel my toes, and my fingers were numb despite thick gloves and hand warmers. The metal of my rifle hurt to touch barehanded and I alternated putting each of my hands in my pocket in hopes I'd be able to pull the trigger when we got to the target.

We were on a winter deployment in 2009. Our intelligence analysts were tracking a group of fighters in a valley south of Kabul. We'd hit a couple of decent targets, but mostly dry holes. The winter deployments were always slow because of the weather. The run-of-the-mill, low-level fighters hung up their guns when it got cold and waited for the spring fighting season.

Our analysts were working on tracking down a very high-level Taliban commander. Using multiple sources, including drones, they were able to locate him. From the drone feed we could see that the commander was traveling with a large group of fighters and they were holed up in a building at the center of a village.

We were told the commander and his fighters were responsible for a series of attacks in the valley that killed several Coalition soldiers. At this point we had collected enough intelligence; we were sure we could get a missile strike approved. After all, there was no reason to go out in the cold and risk our lives in a gunfight if someone could simply push the "easy button" and drop a bomb on him.

But these guys were not your standard Taliban fighters. The commander moved from mosque to mosque and village to village, never staying more than a short time in any place. They had been trained and knew our limitations. The Taliban were getting smarter and smarter at countering our tactics. They knew that with our current rules of engagement we couldn't bomb a mosque or even go inside. Working with this kind of knowledge, they simply never exposed themselves long enough for us to take a shot.

That meant we'd probably have to go out in the dead of winter and hunt them down. Combat was dangerous enough, but even more so in waist-deep snow and freezing-cold temperatures.

SEALs are taught starting in BUD/S to be comfortable being uncomfortable. From drown proofing, where the instructors tie our hands and feet and throw us in the water, to Hell Week, where we spend five and a half days swimming, running, and moving with fewer than four total hours of sleep during the whole week, SEALs experience a lot of un-comfortable conditions.

Part of being a SEAL is overcoming cold, exhaustion, fear, stress, and pain. It is easy to lose focus, drive, and de-termination when things are uncomfortable. We know from early on that not everything we do in the job is going to be comfortable.

Not everything is going to be easy.

During BUD/S training, I concentrated on just getting to the next meal. If I made it to breakfast, I started thinking about lunch. After lunch, I focused on dinner. If I started to think about the weeks and months of uncomfortable chal-lenges ahead of me, I lost focus, so I just didn't.

That was a mind-set that was coming in handy during this deployment. As I trudged toward the village, I broke the mission down into small steps. First conduct the patrol. Then assault the target. Then go home and get warm. But at that moment, I was still on step one. I knew I had to set little goals and reach them. And along the way, I might forget I was miserable.

There is a reason we chose "The only easy day was yester-day" as our motto. We used to joke, "Everyone wants to be a SEAL on Friday." It was easy to be a SEAL at the bar or when you're out with friends relaxing. But being excited about be-ing a SEAL in the middle of winter in Afghanistan when you know you have a long, crazy, cold night in front of you is a different story.

The analysts continued throughout the day watching the

commander move from building to building in the village. As it got dark, his group moved farther up the valley and entered what could be a mosque. From the drone feed, it was kind of hard to tell which mud building among the rest of the mud buildings was indeed the mosque.

I huddled in the operations center with Steve and watched footage of the fighters trudging down a goat trail, moving from compound to compound. As they walked, the last guy in line fell back a little, checking to make sure no one followed. They walked in patrol order; it wasn't the typical gaggle of farmers walking down the road. My eye tracked forward, looking at each fighter in the line until I got to the point man. He was well ahead of the main body and keenly looking for possible Coalition forces waiting to ambush them.

"Let's just bomb these guys," Steve said as we watched the fighters enter the village.

"Can't see any guns," said one of the intelligence analysts. "No guns, no strike. Besides they very rarely clear civilian buildings long enough for us to coordinate an air strike."

We watched helplessly as the fighters filed into what we thought was another mosque. While most of them got warm inside, three stayed outside to keep watch. Two of the fighters started to walk up and down the main road, and a third sat outside of the main entrance to the building. Maybe we couldn't see their guns, but obviously these men were guards. There was no other reason to stay outside in this weather. How often did we find Taliban fighters pulling security without weapons? Never.

My troop chief asked each of us for our assessment.

"What do you think, fellas, can we pull this off?" he said.

We knew the hard truth: If we didn't roger up to conduct this mission, the bad guys would get away. They would go on to conduct more attacks or set IEDs that would in turn kill American or Coalition forces.

"I guess they'd rather send us in, with the possibility of getting one of us shot, than to drop a bomb," Steve said with a short pause and a disgusted look. "We all agree that this is a ripe target. If we don't take a swing at it tonight, we're going to miss them."

Steve paused for a second.

"I'm in."

In a way I was happy. The deployment had been too quiet. We all wanted to get outside the wire. Our job was dangerous, we knew that, but we preferred work to sitting around. Boredom was worse than danger.

Steve and I had been swim buddies a long time and I knew he was doing the same mental checklist I was.

It was a good target. The illumination was low—not zero percent, but close. The enemy was located so far up an enemy-controlled valley they wouldn't be expecting us. Add the freezing-cold temperature, blowing wind, and snow, and you'd have to be insane to attempt this mission. I loved the harder missions. My mind wandered back to the miserable conditions and freezing-cold days spent in Alaska. I'd grown up in these kinds of conditions.

"OK," I said. "Let's do it."

All the team leaders gave him the thumbs-up.

The troop commander and troop chief left the planning to us. Steve and I sat down along with our recce team leader and studied all the possible routes in and out of the village. The target's current position sat at the end of the valley.

There was no way to land our helicopters uphill from the target, and if we landed over the ridge in the next valley, there was no way we would be able to patrol over the extremely steep mountains in waist-deep snow in one cycle of darkness.

Everyone knew the dangers of being caught in the valley when the sun came up. With our small force, we could quickly find ourselves in a very bad position. Plus, there was tons of snow, making any cross-country travel slow and miserable.

We had only one choice: fly in and land well down the valley, far enough away from the village that the Taliban wouldn't hear the noise from our helicopters. The planning wasn't anything special—we were relying on our ability to shoot, move, and communicate. It was pretty basic, and besides, we'd been conducting these types of missions for years at this point in the war. The only thing different tonight was the snow and cold.

I didn't relish the thought of slogging my way up the valley, but my hope was the weather would keep the bad guys inside. We were banking on being the only ones foolish enough to be out.

Helicopters had heaters, but they never worked that well and the ride to the target was a suckfest. We sat huddled together on the jump seats with huge down jackets draped over our shoulders. The trick was to wear just the right amount of layers so that you're not too hot on the patrol when moving, but not freezing once you stop. I had my Arc'teryx jacket and gloves, but nothing on my legs except an extra pair of long underwear. Some of the guys had on Gore-Tex bibs to protect their legs, but I always got too hot in those.

"One minute," I heard the crew chief yell as the ramp of the helicopter began to lower into the open position.

A rush of even colder air entered the cabin as I threw off my large parka.

"This is going to suck," I thought.

I could tell by the howl of the engines that we were close to landing. From the one-minute call until we touched down I always looked out of the window. I tried to gather as much situational awareness of the immediate area as possible. You could never know what piece of information was going to be necessary in a firefight, especially if we were ambushed as soon as we landed.

Tonight, all I could see was white. Snow covered everything, and I could see the moon glistening off the ice. It was beautiful. The snow and mountains of Afghanistan rival some of the best ski slopes in the United States. This place could be a resort if the locals weren't always trying to kill you.

All around me, my teammates shrugged off their jackets and started to work the circulation back into their legs. I moved my rifle into my lap and held on to the crossbar of the seat. This deployment we were working with National Guard helicopters, and their aircraft lacked the high-speed avionics of the special operations squadron. Let's just say their landings weren't the best. We hit the ground with a thud, and I could feel the helicopter's wheels skid as it lurched forward.

From my position looking out the open ramp of the helicopter, it seemed as if the ramp was stuck. I refocused my night vision goggles and could see that we'd landed in such a deep snowdrift that the ramp couldn't open all the way. Our recce guys began climbing through the small opening between the top of the ramp and the top of the helicopter.

When we emerged, the air was bitter cold. I trudged through the waist-deep snow to get out of the rotor blast. I looked back to see my teammates dropping off out of the helicopter and into the snow one at a time. The rotor wash blew snow in my face, all over my equipment, and down my neck.

I began to get my bearings and could see our snipers moving into a position out in front of me. Just then, the helicopter powered up, blowing a second batch of snow down my neck. I stood in place, not moving until the snow subsided and the helicopter noise faded. Up ahead, the snipers started to break trail. Thankfully they'd remembered their snowshoes. The snipers started stamping down the snow so we could walk off the drop zone.

I just wanted to walk.

I knew from my childhood growing up in Alaska that movement was the best way to fight the cold. When we finally got on the road, I started to warm up. I looked back over my shoulder and saw the long line of men, dark against the fresh white snow, snaking its way to the road. Besides my troop, we had a group of Rangers and some Afghan commandos with us.

The moon hadn't set yet, and there was a decent amount of moonlight, so looking through our night vision the landscape was super bright. Above me, the stars seemed to go on forever. Is this what "the Chosin Few" in Korea felt like?

"The Chosin Few" were UN troops, mostly Marines, who fought in the Battle of Chosin Reservoir during the Korean War. It was legendary in our circles. The Chinese encircled the UN troops, who fought for seventeen days in ice and snow before breaking out of the encirclement.

The weather and terrain in some ways were more hostile than the enemy. Temperatures at night bottomed out at thirty-five degrees below zero and just barely reached zero during the day. Food rations froze. Vehicle engines refused to start after being shut down. Marines suffered from frostbite.

It made this march look easy.

During the Korean War they didn't have the cool-guy, top-of-the-line Arc'teryx gear that we had. That's how I rationalized it in my mind. I knew I couldn't bitch about it; plenty of soldiers in the past suffered through much worse.

The crystal-clear night only made it colder. There were no clouds to trap even the smallest amount of heat. I slid one hand at a time into my pocket. My fingers reached for the balled-up chemical hand warmer I carried.

For three hours we patrolled up the valley and toward our target. The march was just plain miserable. The weather was more brutal than even my worst days in Alaska riding on the back of my father's snow machine. There was no avoiding it. My fingers stiffened each time I took them out of my pocket. Gusts of wind blew snow into my face.

Up ahead, I could see enormous wisps of snow blowing off the top of the mountains that towered over the end of the valley. With every gust, I had to make a conscious effort to focus on the mission and not the cold. We were deep within an enemy-controlled valley, outnumbered, and our assessment said we were heading toward some pretty hard-core fighters.

Over the radio, the drone pilots were still reporting just the three guards. The rest of the fighters were holed up in the building.

"The warm building," I thought.

We took a quick break and one of my teammates gave me an Atomic Fireball candy. My feet were numb from the cold and I was reluctant to even take my gloved hand out of my pocket to accept it.

"Maybe it'll warm me up," I thought as I popped it in my mouth.

At the very least, it would keep my mind on the burning sensation on my tongue and off my cold feet. When things get miserable, especially this miserable, the only thing to do is laugh about it. The roads were icy and very slick. Every five minutes or so, one of the guys in the patrol would slip and crash to the ground. I laughed to myself each time, until I hit a slick patch. My foot instantly started to slide and I knew I was going down.

Wham.

I was on my ass looking up at the stars. I could feel the cold snow soaking my pants. A few guys snickered as I scrambled to my feet. Karma is a bitch.

We made it to the ORP—the observation ready point— three hundred meters from the target, where we stopped to make any last-minute adjustments to the plan and get prepared to assault the target. I slid my hands reluctantly out of my thick winter gloves and into my thin shooting gloves. I could feel the cold metal of my weapon through the material. I blew on my fingertips and flexed them back and forth, hoping to get the blood moving so my trigger finger would work.

I gathered with the troop commander, troop chief, Steve, and the other team leaders to make sure there were no last-minute changes. Behind me, my teammates, the Rangers, and the Afghan commandos all took a knee and waited. Two soldiers from the closest base—battle space owners—were with us to handle the village elders after we left. They had gotten on the helicopters at the last moment dressed in their standard-issue cold-weather gear. I could see them nearby shivering and looking around, waiting to move again. If I was cold, these poor fuckers had to be nearly frozen.

There was a sense of urgency to get moving again as soon as possible. As we confirmed our last-minute assault plans, word came down that the building where the fighters were hiding was indeed a mosque. That automatically changed everything. I could hear the troop commander over his radio trying to work out if we would be allowed to enter and clear the mosque or if only the Afghan commandos could go inside. We knew the bad guys were there, and we knew the bad guys purposely stayed in mosques because they knew Americans weren't allowed inside.

After walking for more than three hours, I was sweaty, and the sweat was starting to cool. I'd ditched my warmest gear to prepare for the assault. I didn't want to fish it all out again for fear we'd get the green light to go and I'd have to put it all away a second time.

As the wait dragged on, people started coming up to where the troop commander, troop chief, and team leaders were meeting. At first, it was the Afghans. We often used a SEAL officer to supervise the Afghan commandos. The officer showed up at the ORP with the Afghan commander. He looked exasperated.

"I couldn't get him to stop; they want to know what's going on," the officer said.

"Settle down and relax. We'll tell you when we're ready to go. Now, get back to your positions and we'll let you know," the troop commander said.

Then the Ranger captain came up and kneeled next to me.

"Hey, what's going on?" he asked. "What are we doing?"

"They're in a mosque," the troop commander said. "Just hang tight. We're figuring it out and will let you know when we're ready to go."

The Ranger platoon leader went back without a word. I was getting pissed. I knew everyone was freezing. I was too, but now, only three hundred meters from the target, was not the time to start questioning things. Our troop commander and chief were both working the radios trying to get approvals so we could continue the mission.

The voice of the drone pilot over my radio finally shook me from my thoughts of a warm tropical beach somewhere.

"We've got movers," the pilot said. "They just left the mosque headed north out of the village."

"Roger," the troop commander said. "Can you identify weapons?"

Since the enemy patrol was leaving the village, maybe now we could get an air strike. We'd patrolled through the freezing-cold weather for most of the night, but there was still no need to get into a gunfight if there was an easier way.

"Negative," the drone pilot came back. "We can't identify any weapons."

I looked at Steve and almost laughed.

"Could there be anybody else except bad guys out here at three in the morning in patrol formation?"

Steve looked angry.

"They just left a mosque," Steve said. "They've correlated the group to the Taliban commander. Three guards have been out all night. What the fuck is wrong?"

As bad as we all wanted to go get these guys, we all knew the inherent danger of getting into a shootout. We were putting ourselves at significant risk because we weren't being allowed to drop bombs.

We weren't even sure why they decided to move. Had some early-warning network alerted them? Sure we had landed miles away from the target to avoid the enemy hearing the noise from the helicopter, but who is to say there weren't more Taliban farther down the valley who'd heard us land and called their buddies up the valley? The only benefit was we didn't have to worry about getting approvals to enter the mosque anymore.

My blood was pumping now, so I didn't feel the cold. One hundred percent of my attention and focus was on making sure my team was moving, alert, and in the best tactical position. Walking into a gunfight can warm the blood. The long, cold walk to the target was now over, and it was time to focus on the hunt.

We made the call to go. We quietly maneuvered into the village, careful to make little noise. There was no need to wake up the whole village at the last second. The gate to the mosque was unlocked. The Afghans went in first and started to clear. The Americans—Rangers and SEALs—stayed outside and waited.

The search took a few minutes, and the Afghans didn't find anything. We didn't really expect anybody to be left inside, but we weren't about to pass it by without checking.

Overhead, the drone was keeping track of the fighters as they picked their way up a nearby hill. Again, our request to hit them with a missile or bomb was denied. No visible weapons. We had no choice but to pursue them and deal with the situation accordingly.

After close to four hours of walking, we were not only cold but also tired. I could tell it was taking a toll on the Afghan commando unit that was with us. They weren't being proactive and we had to order them to pull security. They weren't focused on the mission. They wanted to go home.

Our snipers found the enemy's trail and we slowly started the chase. After about a half hour of moving, the drone pilots once again reported in that the Taliban patrol had come to a building and stopped. Hopefully bedding down for the night.

At least one guard was positioned on a little saddle overlooking the valley.

The only approach to the new target was between the saddle and a small knoll. As we moved into position and began slowly making our way toward the target, the Taliban guard spotted us. I was near the front and watched the guard stand up and stare at us for a long second. I could see an AK-47 slung across his chest. He then turned and tore ass toward the house where his buddies were sleeping.

The radio traffic cracked in my ear.

"We have multiple movers," the drone pilot said. "I say again, we have multiple movers."

We were in the low point of the saddle. We needed to get to the high ground as quickly as possible. Sprinting up the snow-covered hill, I led my team to the end of a line of compounds opposite where the fighters were running. I was no longer cold. There was no doubt we were about to get into a fight.

The snipers, at the front of the formation, were already set up. As I got up to the knoll, I could hear their rifles firing. I saw two fighters in a dead sprint attempting to run down an adjacent knoll. Our snipers dropped them like rag dolls from more than one hundred and fifty yards away. The rest of the fighters stopped running and dove for cover.

I moved my team farther up the knoll looking for a way to flank the enemy. Our snipers were in place and had the enemy pinned down and unable to escape. The Rangers had now made their way to the top of the knoll and were stacked up on the back side of the hill behind the line of compounds.

I grabbed the Ranger captain.

"Hey," I said. "Your guys want to have some fun?"

I took the captain up to the crest of the hill and told him to set up his machine guns and lay down a base of fire on the enemy position. The Rangers carried the heavier belt-fed machine guns and ammo, and I knew they would love to lighten their loads and get in some action.

The Rangers set up with their machine guns and grenade launchers. I shouldered my rifle and aimed my infrared targeting laser at the enemy location, marking them for the Ranger platoon.

"We're going to flank right and I'll hit you up on the radio when it's time to lift your fire," I said. "Until then, fuck 'em up."

Before I even got off the knoll, I could hear the rattle of the machine guns and thump of grenades. Nobody likes carrying the big guns until you need them. It was an awesome sound as the Rangers laid down covering fire that would hopefully keep the enemy busy as my team flanked their position.

"We have squirters moving on your left," the drone pilot said over the radio.

The snipers stayed in position and focused on the enemy to our front, while Steve's team maneuvered to intercept the movers to our left. My team, with the combat dog, or "hair missile," and the troop chief, continued to move around from the right to eliminate the small pocket of enemy still remaining in the house. We had a perfect "L"-shape ambush on the enemy position.

With the deep snow and uphill terrain, it took us a few minutes to move into position. We crept down toward the building. Our hope was that their attention was focused on the fire coming from the Rangers and our snipers and they wouldn't notice us approaching from their left flank. Up ahead, I could see the Rangers' tracer rounds racing across the small valley and smashing into some small shrubs and trees. Without night vision, it looked like lasers in a science fiction movie.

We pushed the "hair missile" out in front of us as we made our way down the small hill and closed in. It felt like we were about to walk directly into the Rangers' tracers when my troop chief got on the radio and had them cease-fire.

Above me, I heard the familiar hum of the AC-130's engines. We were "troops in contact," which is a fancy way of saying "under fire." All the aircraft that had previously said they couldn't drop bombs were now trying to get in on the action.

It's funny how that works.

Steve and his team were using the AC-130 to take out the squirters. I could hear Steve calling for fire. About a minute later, the roar of the plane's guns echoed down the valley.

The quiet valley was no longer calm. It had become almost deafening with the sound of automatic weapons fire and close air support. Our position was now quiet. No one spoke. We all were focused ahead. I saw the dog zigzag its way forward, sniffing at the snow, looking for a scent. To my right, I could hear my troop chief on the radio coordinating with our troop commander.

So far, we hadn't found any fighters. The snow was deep and it was hard to walk. I had my night vision goggles down and strained to see any movement. My eye never lingered for more than a second on anything. I scanned ahead of me before shifting my gaze closer to make sure I didn't miss anything at my feet. This was the first time I actually felt comfortable on this mission.

Then, from my right I heard a burst of suppressed fire.

POP, POP, POP.

I spun around and caught the troop chief's last few shots as he backpedaled away. In the snow at his feet, I could see what looked like a dead fighter. The troop chief was startled.

"Motherfucker," the troop chief mumbled under his breath.

The troop chief wasn't usually in the front with the assault teams. Since we had so many moving pieces, he was moving along with us. His job was more coordinating and talking on the radio, so when the fighter stirred directly in front of him, he was caught off guard.

From what I could tell, it looked like the fighter might have been wounded in the initial fight and simply hidden in his position and waited to ambush anybody that approached.

He was lying so still the troop chief didn't see him and almost stepped on him.

We continued clearing down the knoll, step-by-step, through the knee-deep snow. As we closed on a small group of buildings, I saw the body of another fighter. I slowly walked over, my rifle aimed at his back. Another SEAL teammate rolled him over, while I covered him. The fighter was dead, machine gun rounds having torn open his chest.

In a small cluster of bushes, we found another body. He was crumpled facedown in the snow, his AK-47 nearby. We found three more bodies nearby for a total of five fighters at our location. The initial barrage from our snipers and the covering fire from the Rangers had done the job.

Once Steve and his team were done calling in close air support from the AC-130, the silence was eerie. I could hear Steve on the radio. His team had killed two fighters. All around us, the Rangers set up security while we combed the bodies for intelligence. We searched through the fighters' pockets, looking for anything that could lead us to another target.

All of the fighters were loaded down with chest racks full of magazines, grenades, and even medical kits. These weren't your standard farmer-by-day, Taliban-fighter-by-night types. They had good equipment and looked like they had maintained it well. They were pipe-hitting, trained, and well-equipped fighters.

Once we were sure the target area was secure, we walked the two conventional Army battle space owners around and showed them each dead fighter and their weapons. This was one of the formalities required under the current rules of engagement. While they took pictures and notes, we gathered up the fighters' weapons and gear and destroyed them with explosives.

The patrol back to the landing zone went by faster. Everyone in the Taliban-controlled valley was up now, and we didn't want to stay around any longer than we had to. It was only a matter of time before more fighters came out to avenge their dead friends.

It was still very cold out and we were all sweaty from the firefight. My shirt was soaked and my pants clung to my skin. The difference was for the patrol out of the valley, my mind was on the fact that we'd successfully eliminated the entire Taliban element. They would never harm any American service members again.

I slid my winter gloves on and pulled my beanie down over my ears before replacing my helmet on my head. When the troop chief gave the order to move, we moved out without a word. I kept putting one foot in front of the other, thinking about the warm shower back at the base. I hoped the showers still had hot water.

The mission doesn't always wait for sunny, seventy-two-degree days. Whether the objective is in waist-deep snow, the middle of the shark-infested Indian Ocean, or up a goat trail in the highest peaks of Afghanistan, we are trained to stay focused and complete the mission. We don't need comfort to be effective.

BUD/S seems sadistic to outsiders, but it is where we start

to condition ourselves to not only get comfortable with discomfort, but also embrace it. On Friday evenings the instructors lined us up on the sand at the edge of the water.

"Everyone wants to be a SEAL on Friday," the instructor would yell. "It's Friday and you're all going to have the weekend off. You're going to hit the bars and relax. The question is, which one of you wants to be a SEAL when the conditions are shitty? Which one wants it when you're wet, tired, cold, and miserable and you still have to complete your mission?"

No one spoke. No one smiled. We just wanted to go for the weekend.

"Look to your left and right," the instructors would say. "Will they be there when the going gets tough?"

The whole time the instructors kept walking the line.

"The only easy day was yesterday, gentlemen. You think about that this weekend, and when you start training again on Monday, just know that it's going to suck much worse than it did today." I can honestly say, I've been colder and more miserable than any situation they put us in during BUDs. The saying holds true: "The only easy day was yesterday."

CHAPTER 11
Watch the Shoes

Evolution

I got the page early in the morning.

Team leaders in the squadron always carry small black pagers on deployment so planners can alert us of a possible mission. I rolled out of my lumpy bed, which was built into the wooden walls of my room, and headed over to the operations center.

We were on vampire hours, so while to us it was early morning, really it was a late winter afternoon in Afghanistan. We slept all day and ran missions at night. Things were slow. We'd been at a base south of Kabul for months, with few missions. The bitter cold made the winter fighting season slow. The Taliban were across the border in Pakistan or lying low in Afghanistan. Neither side really wanted to fight.

I stuffed my hands into my jacket as I walked over to the operations center. I had no idea what was going on, and I didn't wake my team. We'd been conducting missions like this for years now, and I knew things could spin down as quickly as they had spun up. Many times we would wake everyone up to start planning and the target would disappear. It was better that they get as much sleep as possible.

I walked into the operations center. It was a squat, prefab building. The floors were muddy from all the dirt tracked in by our boots. There was a worn path from the door to the coffee maker. I followed the track and got a hot cup. I took two quick sips and let the caffeine shake me from my funk.

There was a subdued energy in the room as the planners and intelligence analysts pored over data, trying to tee up that night's mission. Black-and-white Predator feeds trained on a compound were displayed on the screen. Standing near the back next to a long desk were the troop chief and troop commander. They saw me come in and nodded. I dropped three packets of sugar into my coffee and joined them.

"What's up?" I said.

"ISR has been tracking some fighters," the troop chief said.

The drones patrolling overhead caught a group of five to seven fighters going from compound to compound, looking for a warm bed and meal. They'd been moving most of the day but had just stopped. The planners figured the group was going to stop moving and bed down at the compound for the night. It was starting to get dark and they'd been traveling most of the day.

"From what we can see from the ISR, it looks like they were just walking through town and decided to hide out at this random house for the night," the troop chief said. "We saw them knock on the door and when the people inside answered they pushed through the door. They even moved their vehicles inside the compound's wall."

I was one of three team leaders. I looked over at Steve as the troop chief gave us details on the compound's location. Steve was nodding as the troop chief told us about the mission.

After the first briefing, the recce team leader started working up routes to the house. I started looking at the house with Steve.

"Looks pretty cut-and-dry to me," I said.

"I agree. You going to wake up your crew?" Steve said.

"Yep, I'll wake them up now so they can grab some food before we start spinning too hard," I said.

I followed the muddy path to the door and made a beeline to where the guys were sleeping. The tent was pitch-black. Only a small strip of white rope lighting ran down the hallway toward our makeshift lounge area. The plywood walls separated the tent into little mini-rooms, each with a bed and desk. Each room had one SEAL. It was tight quarters, but at least you had some privacy.

The far end of the tent was the lounge. It was spacious, with stadium seating in front of a fifty-inch flat screen. We'd been coming to Shank for years, and each squadron worked hard to make the living conditions a little better each time. A previous squadron built a fire pit and outdoor lounge. Another fixed up the gym. If we had to do time in Afghanistan, the goal was to make it as nice as possible.

I turned on the light in the lounge and turned the TV on. We could watch the American Forces Network, which broadcast American shows, movies, and sports. But we'd also rigged it to show the same ISR feed that the planners saw in the operations center. I turned on the feed. All around me, I could hear the boys stirring. Guys were getting out of their bunks.

I put on a pot of coffee. One by one, with a fresh cup in their hands, the guys gathered around the TV. There was nothing to see other than the compound walls and buildings. There was no movement inside the walls or near the compound because the fighters had already moved inside the buildings.

"Sweet," Walt said. "Same shit, different day."

He rubbed his eyes and watched the black-and-white picture for a few seconds.

"This better not be another dry hole. I don't go out in these temperatures for less than twenty bad guys," Walt said in his typical smartass tone.

Once all the guys got a cup of coffee or a drink, I started the brief. I gave them the rundown on the target and the fighters. There was nothing difficult about this hit. We'd rolled up fighters sleeping in compounds just like this hundreds of times before. In many ways this mission was just plug-and-play. Everyone knew what roles needed to be filled.

Our plans were always pretty simple, but I tried to give my guys a chance to shoot holes in it. I started with the basic questions.

What are we missing?

Does what the intelligence folks are saying match with what we are seeing?

What were everyone's responsibilities for the night?

Which team would lead the assault?

Everyone on the team had input, even the newest guy. I knew I definitely wasn't the smartest guy in the room, and I had learned a long time ago to ask for outside opinions.

It took about an hour to get everything in place. When we were done, Steve and I went back to the troop chief and briefed the plan. The troop chief and troop commander sat in the operations center listening carefully as we detailed the routes to and from the target and the assault plan.

Although our intelligence analysts were confident the fighters were not going to move again the rest of the night, we kept a watchful eye on the compound. The drones kept a constant vigil overhead.

We planned to land about five kilometers from the target and patrol to the compound. This allowed us to keep the element of surprise. Nothing gives away your position like a massive helicopter hovering above. With the high mountain peaks and long valleys, the helicopter noise would float for miles and everybody up and down the valley would know we were coming. Sometimes we'd land one valley over in order to keep the rotor noise down. The only problem with that idea was you had to walk your happy ass up and over a mountain.

I watched the troop chief and troop commander carefully as we briefed. They nodded their heads as we laid everything out. The plan was simple, so I didn't anticipate any issues. The troop commander blessed off on the plan, and a couple hours later we were airborne, headed to the compound.

I was excited as I sat in the Chinook, trying to think

warm thoughts. In the back of my mind I wasn't nervous about anything. I was confident, not arrogant, that I knew how to handle almost anything on target. By my thirteenth deployment, I was light-years ahead of my first missions. I'd come a long way from the kid in a T-shirt hoping to be a SEAL. I'd learned valuable lessons on the streets of Baghdad on my first combat deployment.

There was no stopping a lucky shot or well-placed road-side bomb, but after thirteen deployments there was little that surprised me. I'd been sent to a compound rigged to explode when I arrived. I'd walked into countless houses in Iraq and Afghanistan and faced fighters waiting to ambush me. The missions weren't any easier, but I had a wealth of experience behind me.

Part of the reason my teammates and I were so capable was we constantly tried our best to evolve. The enemy was always changing their tactics, and if we didn't change ours as quickly, we would fall behind, putting ourselves at risk.

At the start of the war in Afghanistan, few of us had seen any real combat. We were highly trained with no experience, but after a decade of war, almost ninety percent of the force had real-world combat experience and close to double-digit deployments under their belts.

During every deployment, we pushed to change tactics and techniques as quickly as our enemy did. We never rested on what worked in the past; instead we pushed to develop what would work in the future.

I closed my eyes and let the hum of the helicopter's engines wash over me. Some of my teammates were already asleep. I rested my eyes and went over the mission in my head. I tucked my hands between my body armor and my stomach, trying to keep them as warm as possible for as long as possible. It wasn't Alaska cold that night, but it was still cold enough that I could feel it through my gloves.

We were used to this routine. At this point in the war and our careers, we had become somewhat numb to the pain, suffering, and sacrifice of going on missions. I rationalized it all as "just part of the job." Some people had chosen different professions, but this was ours and we were getting really fucking good at it.

I felt the helicopter dip down and heard the engine pitch change as it landed. A mix of dust and snow greeted us as we dashed off the back ramp. I got about fifty yards from the helicopter and started to piss into the dirt. I'd been holding it for the hour-long flight and I knew once we got moving I wouldn't have a chance to go. All around me my teammates were doing the same thing. As the helicopter's engines faded away, we got into patrol formation and started toward the compound.

No words had to be spoken. No order given. This was another day at work for us. Everyone knew what to do, where to go, and what was expected of him. Sure the bureaucracy and bullshit rules from senior officers were always there, but we always worked with them and around them and otherwise did our best to block it all out of our minds.

In the green hue of my night vision goggles, I could see my teammates spread out before me. We had been patrolling toward the target for about an hour when the radio crackled to life.

"We've got two MAMs [military-age males] coming out of a door on the west side of the compound," I heard over the radio. "They just moved over to a door on the east side."

Shit, the fighters were still awake. If people in the compound were awake, it meant we would have to use different tactics on the assault. We wouldn't be able to silently pick the lock and slowly make our way into their bedroom and catch them by surprise.

As it stood, based off the latest report from ISR, we'd have to call them out, giving up our element of surprise and allowing them time to arm themselves to make a stand. I'd been around long enough to know that folks who really had no clue what was happening on the ground made most of the rules we operated under.

But we still had a long walk ahead of us. I hoped by the time we got to the compound the fighters would be asleep. I kept scanning for threats and focused on the long patrol. As we got closer, the ISR pilot was on the radio again.

"The two movers just returned to their original doorway and went inside," the pilot said.

We patrolled over a few small hills and into a thicket of trees near the compound. This was our final set point before we assaulted the target. From the trees, I caught a glimpse of the compound. At night and in the dark, it looked like just another compound in Afghanistan. It had high mud walls and a heavy wooden gate.

Since the last warning, the compound had been quiet.

No movement.

No more sleepwalkers.

We waited a few minutes to make sure no one got up again. Finally, the troop chief made the call to continue with the assault. Because of the freezing temperatures, our troop commander made the decision to sneak over the wall instead of conducting a callout because a callout would only expose the women and children to the bitter cold. Plus, if the Taliban decided to fight, the women and children would be stuck in the crossfire.

We quietly moved into position. My team fell in behind the snipers and we made our way to the front gate of the compound. I watched the snipers scale the walls and set up overwatch positions.

The gate was made of wood with an old iron latch as a handle. The point man tried the latch, but it was locked on the inside. He called to one of the new guys who was carrying the extendable ladder on his back. We placed the ladder against the wall and the point man slowly climbed the giant mud wall. Another ladder was passed to the point man as he straddled the ten-foot-high wall. As we passed the ladder up to him, he seemed to wobble a little and quickly reached down and got his balance.

We were wearing more than sixty pounds of gear and the point man was doing gymnastic-style moves on the top of a ten-foot-high wall with a room full of sleeping Taliban fighters thirty feet away.

Rung by rung, we passed the ladder up. It was tense because silence, not speed, was the most important thing. It was pitch-black outside. The wind was picking up, blowing the ladder around a bit. A few times I was afraid the point man was going to lose his balance and tumble into the compound.

All I could think about was the sleepwalkers. The report was of two movers, but ISR was tracking between five and seven fighters altogether. We all knew which door the two movers had come from and then later gone back into, but nobody knew exactly where the others might be sleeping. If they were to walk through the compound again, the snipers would drop them. But that would likely wake up the other fighters still sleeping inside. My hope was that we could get inside the house before the fighters had any idea we were there.

The point man finally got the ladder up and delicately lowered it into the compound. Then he and his swim buddy climbed down into the compound. I waited by the gate, ready to enter. A few seconds later, I could hear the bolt of the gate slide back, and the heavy wooden door slowly swung open.

The point man stood in the opening with a shit-eating grin on his face.

"Too easy," he whispered.

We now had the front door open and it was time to go to work. We all crept through the gate and into the compound, which opened up into a small courtyard with buildings along the perimeter. Everybody moved as quietly as we possibly could. The "don't run to your death" rule always applied. After all, this wasn't a video game. You can't just get shot and re-spawn in place.

Several of the newer guys were in front of me as we slipped inside the compound. I watched them veer off to search animal pens and the north and east side of the compound. I could tell the younger guys were all amped up. They were doing their best to suppress their energy.

But the key was being in the right place, and after more than a dozen deployments, I knew where the fighters were sleeping by listening to the ISR pilot on the patrol to the target. As I listened to each report, I thought back to the compound layout. The movers came out of a door on the west side of the compound. I headed straight for the west door. If the ISR was correct, the lone door on the west side of the compound was where the fighters were sleeping.

I didn't run.

I wanted to be not just slow, but super slow. Slow is smooth and smooth is fast. I moved over to the west side of the compound and waited by the closed door. One of the new guys on his first deployment with the troop was on the other side of the door. I reached out and pressed the door handle down. The door was unlocked.

The door opened inward into a small anteroom. Two wooden doors were on either side of the room. A staircase leading to the second floor of the house was almost directly in front of us. Since I opened the door, the new guy was the point man and would be the first person to enter. He slowly stepped inside and I followed.

I saw from the doorway a whole bunch of men's shoes in a pile next to the right door. The pile was a mix of big leather sandals and black Cheetahs. We joked that we'd never seen an innocent person wear a pair of Cheetahs. The black shoes equaled Taliban more times than not.

The opposite door had kids' and women's shoes stacked outside. I knew the instant we walked inside the anteroom where the fighters were sleeping. But the new guy, probably a little too amped to notice, went to the left door. I moved to the door on the right. As I reached for the knob, I was one hundred percent sure the fighters were inside the room. My hope was they were sound asleep.

The beat-up, rusty, old hinges let out a long squeak. In the silence, it sounded like a freight train barreling through the mud hut. The room was freezing and it was pitch-black inside. I had my night vision goggles down and could make out man-sized lumps lying under blankets.

As I scanned around the room, a fighter just to the left side of the door stirred and sat up. He was about three feet away from me. He must have heard the door and was trying to make me out in the darkness. Looking beside him, I spotted a large belt-fed PKM machine gun. His vision quickly cleared. He could tell whoever was at the door was not friendly. His hands instantly shot out and he grabbed the machine gun. The problem for him was the PKM's barrel was pointed away from the doorway.

I watched for a split second as he wrestled with the gun, trying to get it turned and facing my direction. He never got the chance. I leaned in and shot him twice in the face.

My rifle had a suppressor, but even the muffled shots seemed loud in the mud room. The fighter flopped backward like he was going back to sleep and disappeared from view. I raised my rifle to cover the rest of the room and saw AK-47 rifles leaning against the wall. Chest racks stuffed with magazines hung on the wall. The "lumps" under the blankets immediately turned into a blur of movement as all the fighters woke up and scrambled to get their guns.

I didn't hesitate.

I started to shoot. Tracking from one fighter to the next, I pumped two or three rounds into each blur's chest, pausing only for a second to make sure the fighter went down. There was no yelling or screaming, just the muffled sound of my rounds cutting into the enemy fighters.

The fighters crumpled or fell back to where they had been sleeping. Each shot sent a charge through the dark wool blankets, which looked like a wave rippling over a lake. As quickly as it began, it ended. I stepped into the room with a swim buddy behind me and we moved from fighter to fighter, making sure they were no longer a threat.

There were six fighters total. I counted five AK-47s and one PKM machine gun. We also recovered two RPGs and several rockets. The fighters were well armed. Their guns were in decent shape and they had good gear compared to a typical Taliban fighter. We also found first aid kits and Afghan and Pakistani money.

No shots were fired in any rooms other than the room I cleared. All of the fighters had huddled into the one room. The family living there likely had no choice but to let the fighters hole up inside their home.

As I consolidated the weapons, I could hear the women and children crying across the hall. As I predicted, the new guy had walked into the women's sleeping room. They were startled when he walked inside. When I started shooting, they started to scream. When I left the room I'd cleared, I poked my head into the opposite room and saw him pulling security on a room full of unhappy women. He didn't look thrilled.

Just before we started to patrol back to the helicopter landing zone to catch our ride home, the new guy came up to me.

"Motherfucker," he said. "I knew I should have gone to the right."

During a slow deployment, missing a chance to send some rounds downrange was painful.

"Don't be mad at me," I said. "You had first dibs on which door to take."

"I'm not mad at you. I'm just pissed at myself for not catching that sooner," he said.

"Always—I repeat, always—check the shoes," I said.

I'd learned the shoe lesson the hard way on a previous deployment to Iraq. When you're new, all amped up, and in a hurry, you miss the little details, like the shoes, that can be meaningless at first glance but are really a big clue. When you're more experienced and have been in the car crash a million times, and have made mistakes and learned from them, everything slows down and something as small as shoes can stand out.

This time, I read that situation perfectly. In our line of work, you can only hope to survive your first mistake and live long enough to never make it again. Thinking about it now, it was one of many lessons I learned that I still use today. On the practical side, it was about tracking the enemy, but the more universal lesson was about attention to detail in high-stress situations. In this instance, success meant life or death.

This was my thirteenth combat deployment. I had years

of my life spent operating in Iraq, Afghanistan, and all over the world. This was no longer "theory" or "training." For the first time in my career, I felt like I'd achieved my goal of becoming the SEAL operator that I'd dreamed about as a teenager in Alaska.

Years of training had led me to this level. No SEAL I ever worked with was content being average. We'd learned teamwork in BUD/S and we were experts in our individual tactical skills. After more than ten years at war, our skills were at their peak. We'd shot millions of rounds, blown thousands of pounds of explosives, and trained and fought in every situation and environment. We could spin up on an operation on a moment's notice, no matter how complex. Mission planning was simple because we'd done it hundreds of times. We trusted each other and could almost read each other's minds on target.

CHAPTER 12
Killing

Compartmentalization

Even though the command had given us a few days off after returning from the mission, I still found myself back at work. I needed to get back to the same routine as I'd had in past deployments.

I wanted to control something. It was comforting to pull up to the building, go to my cage, unpack all my gear, and zone out for a bit. I really wanted some solitude.

I'd never felt anxiety after a mission. I was always able to handle the stress, but now it was messing with me. I wasn't sleeping. I was on edge. I didn't want to talk to anyone, and I was even dodging calls from my family.

I heard a buddy who was also on the raid open up his cage just down the aisle from mine. The cage area was pretty quiet, so I gave it a second and walked over. He had his gear out and was doing the same thing I had been doing, attempting to hide in his work. He was slowly putting his gear away but looked up when I walked into his cage.

"Hey, bro," I said. "What are you up to?"

"Not much, figured I'd clean up some of my gear," he said.

I could see the thick circles under his eyes. He looked tired. The command is a tough place. To an extent, we're a pack of wolves. A group of alpha males taught to never show weakness. I'd known this guy for years and we'd been in some pretty shitty situations together. I trusted him with my life, but admitting weakness was something else entirely.

"Can I ask you a quick question?" I said softly.

"Sure, what you got?" he said.

"Are you sleeping?" I said in almost a whisper.

He continued to unpack his bags, and after a long pause he looked back up at me.

"Nope," he said.

He shook his head when he said it and then turned away.

"Me neither," I said. "I haven't gotten more than an hour since we got back."

That was the single deepest conversation I ever had about combat stress.

I've been through shooting courses. I can go rock climbing, ride a dirt bike, drive a boat, and handle explosives. The government spent millions of dollars training me to fight in the jungle, arctic, and desert. I took language courses and I can parachute at night and land right on target. But I've never been trained to handle the stress of combat. We spent months learning how to be SEALs and hours of every day keeping those skills sharp, but we got no formal training dealing with any of the emotional stuff.

Before I joined the SEALs, I wondered if I would actually be able to pull the trigger. Could I defend myself? I only really thought about it before I became a SEAL because once I was on missions I didn't have time to think about it. I was in my three-foot world.

Everything I did overseas was considered work. I snuck into people's houses while they were sleeping. If I caught them with a gun, I killed them, just like all the guys in the command. I've been in massive gunfights and I'd put guys down without thinking about it. I don't regret my actions in combat. Everything I did overseas was done to protect the guys to my left and right, and my country. I obeyed the rules of engagement and never targeted innocents.

But that doesn't mean it didn't fuck with me. To this day, if you ask Phil about "the cat," he'll tell this story of a 2006 mission in Iraq.

The unmanned drone flying over the target reported seeing a half dozen men sleeping outside. It was summer in Iraq, and even at night it was too hot to stay inside without air conditioners. The village was really just a cluster of about ten squat, adobe-style houses. I didn't see any power lines coming into the village as we patrolled, so we expected people to be sleeping outside.

We closed slowly on the village just before three in the morning. Since we'd gotten off the helicopter two hours before, it had been a long march to the village. The desert was flat and wide open and it was hard to see the horizon, even with my night vision goggles down. The village could have been on the moon. Nothing surrounded it for miles except sand and rocks. Above me, the stars were thick and bright.

Now, close to the houses, the march was one slow step at a time.

It was 2006 and we'd been fighting in Iraq for three years. My troop was working in western Iraq. A tip brought us to the village. ISR spotted fighters and we spun up. The whole process was pretty simple by this point. We were doing it every day. Find, fix, and finish.

It was hot and I could feel the sweat pooling around my back where my body armor stopped. The troop chief gave the word and we moved into a large "L"-shaped formation and started to close on the village.

The base, or bottom, of the "L" was going to set up just outside of the village and, if needed, provide a base of fire and cover our movement. The vertical part of the "L" was going to move through the village searching for fighters. I was in the second group.

On the radio net in my ear, I heard updates from the other assault teams. I knew that circling above us and just outside of audible range, we had drones to give us eyes in the sky and an AC-130 to cover us in case we needed immediate close air support. I scanned over to where the drones reported seeing the sleepers. I could make out about ten bedrolls.

A pair of men stood, scanning the desert. They weren't talking, or at least it didn't appear so. It looked like they were straining to see into the blackness of the desert night.

Did they hear something?

I was sure they couldn't see us. Maybe they heard the AC-130 above. Finally, one man moved over to where the others were still sleeping and began waking them up. His partner never stopped scanning the open desert. I could see the others getting up, slowly, and start looking around.

While the others got moving, the pair of men walked toward the nearest house. The others eventually followed. None of the men had guns so we couldn't open fire, but it was definitely suspicious to see a large group of men sleeping on the outskirts of the village. Where were all the women and kids?

The group was halfway to a house on the edge of the village when they stopped. The entire group turned and started to walk back to their bedrolls. We were about two hundred meters away and I could see every one of the men clear as day in my night vision.

When they got back to their bedrolls, I could see them grabbing AK-47s, RPGs, and even a belt-fed PKM machine gun. Multiple IR lasers popped on and zeroed in on the chests of the fighters as our snipers went to work. Seconds later, three of the enemy dropped. The others panicked and started running back toward the village. Suppressed rounds continued to pour in on them.

I counted five dead fighters. By this point in the war, we were very conscious of not running to our death, so we paused for a moment. The base of the "L" stayed in place. We were hoping the enemy hadn't noticed the rest of us off to their right flank. Our position hadn't fired yet in an effort to stay undetected.

Within minutes I heard the troop chief's voice over the radio.

"OK, guys, the base is going to hold position and the maneuver is commencing assault at this time."

This meant that the maneuver, or our side of the "L," was going to start slowly clearing our way through the buildings. We'd done this a million times before and the tactic was nothing new. The simple "L" ambush or assault has been used throughout history.

I made a quick check of my gear and took a knee and waited for the order to move.

"OK," I heard the troop chief say over the radio. "Take it."

Our entire element got up and began slowly bounding forward in pairs. Two or three SEALs would slowly make their way forward with guns at the ready, stopping a short distance ahead of the next group. They would then take a knee and hold security while the rest of the unit bounded past them.

It wasn't fast, and I'm sure it wasn't sexy, but it was the safest way to close on the enemy. Especially when we'd already lost the element of surprise.

I could see a few lasers scanning doorways. The natural instinct is to move quickly, but we continued to move at a glacial pace, always ready to open fire at the first sign of trouble. We were just about to enter the village when we saw four men in a dead sprint racing back to the bedrolls.

"Looks like these guys forgot something," I heard over the radio.

These guys must have had balls of steel to attempt a dead sprint back to retrieve their guns, especially since their weapons and bedrolls were now littered with the bodies of their dead friends.

I was less than one hundred yards from them. I raised my gun and zeroed in on the first guy in the group. He looked anxious as they sprinted, his eyes wide. He practically slid to a stop, his chest heaving, and started to root through the folds of his bedroll. The first man got to his bedroll and knelt down. I could see him pull out an AK-47.

I put my laser on his chest and fired. My teammates also opened fire. We all hit the same guy in rapid succession, spinning him down. Our rounds kicked up a little dust cloud, covering the area where the man once stood. I tracked to the next guy, only to watch as he fell forward in a heap. One by one, I followed our lasers to the next target until all four were on the ground, unmoving.

Again, we paused to assess the situation.

I took a knee and began scanning the surrounding buildings, waiting for any more "heroes." Phil, my team leader, took a knee next to me, and I could hear him whisper.

"That was interesting," he said. "I guess they really want to fight. Let's take it slow and careful tonight. These guys mean business."

"Let's keep moving," the troop chief interrupted over the radio.

Phil and I got up and continued moving toward the closest building. I stopped at the doorway and waited. Phil squeezed my arm to signal me to go inside. The house was small, with a foyer leading to a single room. The house was muggy inside, and I didn't see anything as I scanned the room. A rug covered the tile floor and a ratty sofa sat at one end. I could hear my teammates moving into the kitchen just off the foyer.

I quickly moved through the main room and entered a sleeping room. No one was inside, but I could see mats and pillows on the floor. The house was deserted.

"One building clear, at least fifteen more to go," I thought as we started toward another house.

Maybe the house was empty because the civilians that lived there left when the fighters showed up. Or maybe it was connected to the fighters and they'd fallen back and were still waiting for us in the dark. I cleared my head and tried to focus back on the task at hand.

My team spent the next thirty minutes clearing house after house. I was behind Phil later as we walked up the road. The village was a maze and we hadn't run into any more fighters. We knew they hadn't just disappeared. They had to be there somewhere. I scanned every doorway and window, watching for a fighter to pop out.

Up ahead, I caught a glimpse of a guy peering out of a door. He was tucked back in the doorway, but not far enough. I could see the muzzle of his AK-47 as he waited for us to come closer. Thankfully it was dark. At least it was dark to him. We had our night vision goggles.

I wasn't sure Phil saw him at first. The man pulled his head back quickly and I saw Phil's laser shine on where his head once was. The man slowly slid his head back into view as he attempted to get a look at our position. Phil's laser was now on the man's forehead.

I heard several suppressed shots from Phil's MP7, and the man's head disappeared from view.

I held security on the road and additional buildings as Phil and the rest of the team entered the doorway where the fighter once stood. The house was on the far side of the group of buildings we'd just cleared.

I looked back at the door after Phil and the team went inside. I could see the Iraqi fighter's feet in the doorway. Over the radio, I could hear my teammates working with the AC-130 to track down two squirters.

Two fighters ran through the village, popped out the other end, and tried to hide by running out into the open desert. They stood out immediately on the infrared cameras carried by the ISR and AC-130. A team of four SEALs and a combat dog raced out of the village after the fighters. The AC-130 banked and headed toward the group. I was keeping track of their progress on the radio. Finally, I heard the thump of the AC-130's guns.

When my teammates got to the bodies, it was a shocking scene. It looked like one of the fighters was blown completely inside out. A round from the plane's one-hundred-and-five-millimeter howitzer must have hit him. The one-hundred-and-five-millimeter shell is twice the size of a bowling pin, and it can do some serious damage.

Back in the village, I was still holding security when Phil's voice came over the net.

"Alpha Two, Alpha One," Phil said, using our call signs. "Need you in here."

I keyed my radio.

"Roger," I said. "Coming in."

I stepped over the fighter's body and saw Phil and two of my teammates searching the main room. The gun the fighter had been holding was leaning against the far wall of the foyer. Phil had taken the magazine out and cleared the chamber.

I looked back at the dead fighter. His head was lying away from the doorway leading to the main room. Had the fighter not exposed himself in the doorway, there was a good chance neither Phil nor I would have seen him. If he'd had a little patience, he would have had the jump on us.

Phil had clearly popped him with a great shot. The bullet hit him just above his nose, flush in the bottom of his forehead. Half of his face was torn off, leaving one good eye staring blankly at the ceiling. Blood was slowly pooling up around the back of the fighter's head.

I started to look away when a flicker of movement caught my eye. A ratty-ass-looking calico kitten, its fur matted to its skinny rib cage, was at the edge of the blood pool. I have no idea where it came from, but it wasn't uncommon to see cats prowling around the villages in Iraq. The kitten sniffed at the pool, and then I saw its pink tongue dart out and lick the blood.

I expected to see dead bodies, and I had more or less gotten used to it by this point, but there was something about the ratty cat and the blood that didn't seem right. I didn't expect it. It was pretty fucking gruesome.

I turned away and started to search the house. I saw a doorway just off the foyer and stepped through it. It led to a small hallway, and I walked through it into the kitchen.

Pots were stacked on the counter in haphazard piles. The whole room smelled of cooking oil and spices. A hole in the ground for the cooking stove was positioned in one corner. I started to move the pots, looking for weapons or anything left by the fighters. The area was secure, so I wasn't quiet. I was digging through a cabinet near the door when I heard something behind me.

It sounded like a sob or a whimper.

I swung around, one hand on the grip of my rifle, and saw a small child huddled in the corner. He was balled up behind a pile of blankets, and my teammates must have missed him in the initial clearance. I squatted down to get a better look at him. I wasn't sure if he was injured. His hair was matted. His tears washed away some of the dirt from his cheeks. He looked as ratty as the cat licking blood in the foyer.

I looked back over my shoulder and realized that from his vantage point, he would have seen the man in the foyer as he was shot. I had no idea if the man was his father or just a fighter hiding in the house. Either way, he'd watched us shoot the guy and probably saw the cat licking the puddle of blood.

"Wow, I've seen some crazy shit, but this poor kid is going to be fucked up by this the rest of his life," I thought.

The kid was shaking he was so scared. He probably thought we were going to kill him too. Plus, I figured with all of my guns and gear strapped to me, I looked pretty menacing.

The kid continued to quietly sob. I slowly slid a chemlight out of my vest and popped it. The stick slowly lit as I shook it, bathing the room in a green hue. I also slid out a Jolly Rancher and held it out to him. The kid wouldn't look me in the eye at first.

I shook the chemlight.

"Hey, buddy," I said. "I'm not going to hurt you."

I knew he had no idea what I was saying. My only hope was he got my tone. Slowly, he looked up. He was sizing me up, trying to gauge if I was a threat. I tried to smile, but I knew in all my gear a smile wasn't going to be enough.

He looked away and then quickly snatched the chemlight and candy. He didn't eat the candy; instead he just clutched it in his hand. I got on the radio to figure out where we were consolidating all the women and kids. They were in a house not far away, so I stood up and waved at him to follow me.

He didn't move at first.

"Come on, buddy," I said. "I'll take you over to the others."

He didn't understand me, so I took his hand and led him out of the house. I tried to block his view of the dead fighter and the cat, still licking at the pool of blood.

"That was fucked up," I thought. "This kid couldn't be older than five years old and he witnessed the whole thing."

We walked through the village. I could hear a few of the women and kids sobbing when I got to the house. A teammate was at the door keeping watch. When the kid saw the other children and women, he let go of my hand and walked into the middle of the room. I didn't linger. I had work to do and I knew the kid was safe now.

As I walked back to the house to continue my search, I could still picture the cat licking the blood, and the kid watching from across the room as the man's head was blown off. But I quickly pushed the image out of my mind and resumed my search.

I didn't have time to dwell on it. After missions, I blocked it out. I know some guys who make a big deal about killing. I'd shot people from long distances and shot people at point-blank range. But I always rationalized it this way: If I hadn't shot the enemy, he would have killed one of my swim buddies or me. I didn't need another explanation.

But that still didn't make it easier when I got back home to the real world.

My first deployments were like drinking from a fire hose. I didn't know the process; I didn't know what to expect. But after thirteen deployments, I got really good at turning things on and off. I compartmentalized the stress and kept it out of my stateside life.

I remember driving home from our base immediately after returning from the Iraq deployment. There was traffic and I almost drove over the median to get around it. In the early days of the Iraq war, we ran cars off the road when Iraqi drivers got in our way. It was suicide to get stuck in traffic in Iraq. Car bombs were a constant threat. Sitting still made you a target. So we tried to keep moving at all times. We also kept other cars away from our convoy. We threw rocks at car windows, cracked windshields, and shot tires out.

But at home, we're expected to forget everything we did to survive overseas. How did I leave it all over there? I don't know. All I know was I got better and better at compartmentalizing things. I simply blocked out a lot of the emotional stuff. I pushed myself through the confusion of living one life overseas and another at home. It wasn't easy.

I had to make a conscious decision to take control of my life. It was a struggle, one I overcame by redirecting many of the lessons I learned from SEAL training. I simply didn't let the effects of combat control me. It was like the Las Vegas commercial: What happened in Afghanistan stayed in Afghanistan. When I came home I never talked about work to people outside of my teammates.

But after the ▮▮▮▮▮▮ mission, I couldn't shake the stress. The mission was spilling out of my mental compartments. As I left the cage after talking to my buddy, I felt better. I felt reassured knowing that others were going through the same mental gymnastics as I was. I wasn't the only one having trouble trying to comprehend all the shit that had gone on since the raid.

A few years earlier the Navy started trying to address combat stress. Their first idea was requiring us to spend a few extra days in Germany on the way home from every deployment. They wanted us to decompress. This was when posttraumatic stress disorder (PTSD) was in the news and officials were clamoring to find a remedy for the uptick in cases.

Before Germany, we'd be home sometimes twenty-four hours after an operation. I'd go from a gunfight overseas and within a day be back in the States at Taco Bell for my routine, two tacos and a bean burrito. It sounds pretty strange, but that stop at Taco Bell was probably me putting up a wall on another compartment in my brain; it allowed me to keep everything separate.

So after the policy change, we stopped in Germany and the command's psychologist flew over to meet us and give us classes on coping with combat stress and reintegration into the civilian world. For the guys with families, the training was focused on going back to the family routine. The funny part was we'd be home for a few weeks, only to head out on our next training rotation, which would keep us on the road for weeks.

The whole Germany decompression idea eventually backfired. It pissed off our families and girlfriends because our deployments were now three days longer. Not to mention we all came home smelling like good German beer.

The command eventually replaced the Germany stop with a new policy. We all had to meet with a command psychologist. We were required to sit down for a single thirty-minute meeting after each deployment. The thirty minutes were used to talk about any issues we might be having. Once I went down with another buddy, Gerry, to knock it out. We weren't buying into this, and it had become just another line item on my to-do list after returning from a deployment. Each person's thirty-minute session had to be complete before they would allow us to take any leave or vacation time. It was something the senior guys blew off, but we were required to go. We knew it was a box that needed to be checked so the Navy could say we were being counseled and trained to deal with the stresses of combat.

It was toward the end of the day when Gerry and I got to the psych office. I don't remember if it was my appointment or Gerry's, but when the two of us walked into the office, the psychologist was taken aback. She was pregnant, about three weeks away from popping. She looked as tired as we did.

"Listen, you don't have much time," Gerry said, pointing at her stomach. "We're going to save you an extra thirty minutes by doing our sessions at the same time."

After thinking about it a minute, she waved us both into her office. Gerry folded his more-than-six-foot-five-inch body into the couch. I took a seat across from the psychologist. She sat in an office chair with a notepad.

"We're going to talk about some stuff, some sensitive things. Are you guys OK with doing this together?" she said.

"Gerry knows everything about me," I said. "And I know everything about him. We're good."

"OK," she said, taking out her pen and starting on some forms.

For most of the thirty minutes she asked us questions about how we were handling stress and if we had any PTSD symptoms. I can remember her handing us a sheet of paper with a list of symptoms on it. I took a second and quickly read down the list. The symptoms included trouble sleeping, avoiding crowds, and keeping your back to the wall in a restaurant.

I chuckled to myself as I finished.

"Holy shit, I think I have every single one of these," I thought.

I didn't live my life differently, but I definitely felt the effects of just about every single symptom.

I smiled at the doctor and didn't say a word.

When Gerry was done, it was my turn to ask some questions.

"Why are we not more fucked up?" I asked. "Why are we not more messed up from the shit that we've seen? You talk about PTSD. Gerry and I have been trained to deal with just about every combat or tactical situation that can be thrown at us, but we've never had one second of training to deal with the emotional side of things."

She nodded.

"The best way I can describe it is BUD/S," she said.

The mental fortitude, the determination and drive you learn in BUD/S, also helps in combat. We're pushed beyond our mental and physical limits in BUD/S. I learned that I could perform well beyond what I thought were my limits. Because of this, the doctor said we were stronger than the average person.

"So the mental toughness I learned and used to get through BUD/S training is the same I use to overcome combat stress?" I said.

The psychologist smiled.

"It isn't that simple," she said. "But BUD/S does help because most of the training is based on mental toughness. It doesn't hurt that SEALs are all like-minded individuals. Each and every one of you volunteered time and time again to be in combat situations."

She was right. I had known early on in my career that I wanted to be in the line of fire. I accepted the risk, but I also knew it was a challenge I wanted to meet head-on. Would I be able to face the stress of combat and not just curl up in a ball? I guess in a way I knew that being able to push yourself beyond your limits was not only a key to being a SEAL, but a key to a successful life.

"So are you saying BUD/S made me stronger? Or BUD/S just weeded out the weak?" I asked.

I stumped her with that one. Before she could answer, Gerry jumped in.

"I think we're just mentally stronger than everyone else on the planet," he said with a smile.

He was obviously fucking around.

Looking back, he was showing the doctor how we dealt with the stress with humor. When the going gets rough, we were always really good at changing the subject. We blocked things out or made light of it and moved on. There was no way that we could comprehend all that we'd seen and done. It was easier to just make a joke and ignore it.

We left the doctor's office after our thirty minutes and never said another word about it. We had checked the box off our list and could now go on leave. Of course, we would get only about two weeks off until it was time to jump back on the speeding train and begin training and deploying all over again.

Over time, I started to sleep better, and there was some comfort knowing I was strong enough to compartmentalize the traumatic experiences I'd had overseas. I still have the list that the doctor gave me. From time to time, I read over it, and I still have every single symptom on the list. From the helicopter crash on the ███████ raid to that small malnourished Iraqi cat licking the pool of blood from the fighter's head, each experience had its own compartment. The symptoms didn't go away even after I got out of the Navy. I just choose to block them out.

We all deal with the stress of combat in different ways. The way that I've dealt with it isn't perfect and certainly isn't for everyone. Being a SEAL is a tough life and career. The sacrifices go far beyond what I'd ever imagined, but if asked whether I would do it all over again, my answer, without hesitation, would be simple.

Yes.

Last Stop on the Speeding Train

On my last day in the Navy, I made the rounds at the command, making sure all my paperwork was complete.

It was a beautiful spring day and I'd already cleaned out my cage and said goodbye to my troop. For the past couple of months, I'd been stressing about the decision. I'd been going hard for thirteen straight combat deployments with no breaks. For the first time in my career, I admitted that I was tired, even exhausted. The pace of constant deployment, training, deployment, and more training had started to take its toll. I always figured I'd make it twenty years in the SEALs or die trying. Getting out was a massive decision and couldn't be made in a vacuum.

I made the decision the same way I would make a choice in combat. I hit up my swim buddies first to test the water. To a man, they all thought I was crazy. I had fourteen years in the Navy and I needed only six more to earn my pension. But my enlistment was up and I had to make a decision. I could either sign up for four more years with one more deployment and then get moved to an administrative job, or get out and take a shot at some sort of regular civilian life.

I'd almost completed my team leader time, which is arguably the best job at the command. The only thing I had to look forward to beyond this position was becoming troop chief. But I'd have to endure at least two years in a training job until then. The war in Afghanistan was dying down, and with the new rules of engagement, we knew that any "good operating" with just the guys on your team was almost completely gone. Deployments were starting to drag on, with little action. I had joined to fight, not sit around.

The command master chief pulled me into his office. He'd heard about my decision to not reenlist and wanted to discuss it with me. He was a great leader with a no-bullshit attitude. He was well respected in the command and I owed him an explanation for why I was leaving.

"So I hear you're done," he said as I sat down.

I nodded.

"I'm cooked," I said. "I feel like if I don't make a move now, I'll be stuck in the Navy with another four-year commitment, and I'm not sure this job is still what I signed up to do."

"I understand," the master chief said. "I've got over twenty years in and even thought about getting out myself on several occasions before my twenty years. You've only got six years left, though, and you're a huge asset to the team. We'd hate to lose you."

I thanked the master chief for the kind words, but I'd made my decision. There wasn't really anything he could say to change my mind.

"I understand what I am leaving," I said. "But this job has

never been about the paycheck. It's never been about the shitty pension I'd get if I made it to twenty years either. I love this job more than anything in the world and have made it my number one priority for almost fourteen years."

He nodded, fully understanding the sacrifices because he had made them as well.

"The war is slowing down, I'd be moved out of my operational squadron after this next deployment, and all the fun would be over," I continued. "I honestly feel like it's time to move on and figure out the next steps in my life. The idea of a vacation and actually being able to choose my own schedule sounds amazing."

We'd all been running hard for years, but the master chief wasn't going to let me out of his office unless I had a plan.

"Do you have some shit set up on the outside? I don't want you to become a bum," he said with a smirk. "I'm not going to give you some bullshit pitch to get you to stay in the teams. I understand where you're coming from and want you to be happy. You've done your fair share of the fighting. Now, get the fuck out of my office and best of luck."

My next stop was with my former squadron commander. He was the first person to welcome us home from our last deployment. He came running onto the plane after we landed and started shaking our hands. After the mission, he became the acting commander.

Getting called to the third deck, where the officers roam, meant I had to change into my uniform and blouse my boots. I changed out of my shorts and T-shirt and used water to smooth my hair out. I then walked upstairs to meet with the commander.

When he saw me, the commander ushered me into his office. As I sat in the chair across from his desk, I took in the massive mahogany furniture and the walls filled with plaques and other memorabilia. I also saw a blue sleeping mattress tucked in one corner of his office.

"What can we do to keep you?" the commander said. "You're one of the leaders in the community. You're going to run this place someday."

I was honored, but I shook my head no.

"It's time for me to move on," I said. "Like I told the master chief. I'm cooked."

The commander didn't want to hear it. He wasn't going to let me get away without a pep talk. He was doing the sales pitch.

"Look," he said. "This is your life. You're like me. I sleep in the office. I'm a warrior monk."

He wasn't kidding. He didn't take vacations or time off. He ground out each day in an attempt to show how hard he was and how dedicated to the mission. I understood where he was coming from, but I'd just done almost fourteen years of that same type of commitment. I just didn't have a nice office to sleep in. Shit, everyone at the command had done that or more.

"Sir, trust me, to some degree I feel like I'm quitting something for the first time in my life," I said.

He didn't reply. I got the feeling he knew I was gone.

There wasn't anything that he could do to get me to stay in the command.

"I've lived a long time by my gut feeling, and right now, my gut is telling me I need to get off this speeding train," I continued.

"OK, well, if we can't change your mind, I understand, and best of luck in the future," the commander said. He was done trying to convince me to stay. To him, I was just another guy who got off the train.

I stood up, shook his hand, and walked back to the cage area. I ran across a handful of my teammates. We'd already talked about my decision, and like the true brothers that they were, they understood and just wanted me to be happy. But I was also an ex-teammate the minute I decided to not reenlist.

"Hey, fucker, shouldn't you be working behind a desk already?" one of my teammates said.

"Yeah, hey, fatty, good luck with those TPS reports," another added.

Their visions of my dismal civilian existence were colored by *Office Space,* a movie that we had watched no less than a thousand times while on deployment. They already had me in a cubicle in a shirt and tie. In the days leading up to my last visit, I was given a plaque with my name misspelled commemorating my service to the squadron and the SEALs.

All of it felt somewhat hollow.

It wasn't my teammates' fault. They were happy for me, but I also knew they were really focused on the next mission or training trip. For more than a decade I'd been honing my skills to be the best SEAL I could be. But that journey was behind me as I walked out of the gate one final time.

I think of it like a surgeon who, after years of training and working in the operating room, became one of the top two hundred and fifty surgeons in the country. Then, with just under fourteen years in practice, he decides to step away and start all over. He just turned in the keys to the operating room after locking it behind him, and started anew.

As I climbed into my truck to drive home, I felt something I'd trained years to control: fear. I was scared. All the questions I left unanswered started to roll around in my head.

What do I do with the rest of my life?

How do I reinvent myself?

What do I fall back on?

Holy shit, what did I just do?

My decision to get out of the Navy was the toughest I've ever made. All my friends were still in the command. They would continue to deploy and make the sacrifice that comes with the job. I felt like I was quitting, and we were taught never to quit. I felt like I was letting my teammates down. As hard as that was, in the back of my mind, I knew I had made the right decision. The hard part was going to be remembering it.

I was worn-out.

I'd put the SEALs and service to my country above all else, including relationships, family, vacations, free time, and a normal life. I hadn't been on a real vacation in years. There were huge gaps in my pop culture knowledge. I couldn't tell you who won the Super Bowl that year or how many comebacks Britney Spears has had.

But, I could tell you the best tactics for taking down a Taliban stronghold. I was extremely good at skydiving, shooting guns, and plenty of other SEAL skills, but few of those skills are in great demand in the civilian world. I had no idea how my skill set would translate outside of the speeding train of the SEAL teams. I'd just walked away from my purpose in life, and now all the skills I needed to survive as a SEAL were obsolete. I had to redefine my life and goals all over again. In a way, I was back in Alaska, but this time I didn't have a dream to guide me.

The book *No Easy Day* was my first step toward a new purpose.

One of the first things my co-writer, Kevin Maurer, and I talked about when we started working on *No Easy Day* was the book *Men in Green Faces* by former SEAL Gene Wentz. The novel inspired me to become a SEAL. I considered the book and many like it to be an essential tool in my quest to become a SEAL. The books were better than a commercial or recruiting poster because they allowed me to experience a SEAL's world firsthand. The same was true for most of my buddies at work. We had all read books about SEALs when we were young.

Phil, one of my mentors and best friends, read the book *Delta Force: The Army's Elite Counterterrorist Unit* by Colonel

Charlie Beckwith, the unit's first commander. When he was done, he wrote Beckwith a letter telling him about his dream of joining Delta.

Several months later, Phil got a reply. The handwritten note encouraged him to always dream big and told Phil he could achieve anything. It was that letter that encouraged Phil to pursue his dream. Beckwith's encouragement put Phil on the path to an amazing career of service.

I wrote *No Easy Day* to encourage young people and share with the world the sacrifices that our servicemen and women face on a daily basis. I wanted people to understand the community, which is made up of people who go into harm's way daily. I wanted to show the human side of the SEALs after months of hero worship from the politicians.

Sitting in my home office, decorated with mementos from my years as a SEAL, under a picture of my BUD/S training class hanging on the wall, I worked on the book until I felt it captured the raid and the culture of the SEAL community perfectly. I wrote the book the same way I was trained, by enlisting the help of friends, family, and swim buddies. My closest friends gave me a lot of advice when I told them I was writing a book. They urged me to do it "right," and not write another navel-gazing battle memoir that focused on me.

"Don't be the douche bag who thinks he's a superhero," one friend told me. "Make sure it's about the team."

Another just laughed at me when I told him.

"Hey, buddy, if the SEAL community can fully back an

action-packed Hollywood blockbuster like *Act of Valor,* I'm sure you'll be fine with a book that pays respect back to the community," he said.

I did my very best to write *No Easy Day* about the team and for the men and women I served with for more than a dozen years. When it was done, I waited for the publisher to announce it. I was the new guy on the team again and I trusted the experts to help me navigate the book launch. When word of the book came out in August 2012, the coverage shocked me. I don't think I realized the storm I was walking into. The demand for the book far exceeded my expectations, but so did the backlash.

I was standing on the tarmac preparing to do a charity skydiving event in San Diego when I got the call. I was doing tandem skydives with folks willing to donate money to the SEAL Foundation for the chance to skydive with a SEAL.

I've been in some stressful situations, but hearing that my name had leaked was in the top ten for sure. For a split second, the stress consumed me. I guess in hindsight I was naïve to think I could maintain my privacy, but I never seriously considered it.

"Well, shit," I thought.

I retreated from the crowd getting ready to jump and took a second to regroup. My training kicked in and I started to make a list of priorities. Skills that I figured were long gone suddenly mattered again. It was like when the instructors pulled off the hood during the hooded box drill. I was back in the box dealing with the situation. Soon, I started to come up with a list of things I needed to do. After the jump, I would start acting on the list.

What could I affect? My name had just leaked. There was no way I could affect anything in the press. I couldn't stuff the words back into the producer's mouth, although I would have loved to meet the Fox News producer and make an attempt with my foot.

First, I had to make sure my parents moved to a safe location away from the prying eyes of the media. Next, I had to limit my personal profile. I was surprised how much information was out there and could be found online. Finally, I stopped worrying about leaks. They were beyond my three-foot world. I had to focus on the things I could change.

One of the organizers of the charity jump waved me over. The plane was ready. I still had to jump. I'd made a commitment to the charity and wasn't about to leave them hanging. I took the stress of the book and the current media situation and put it away, walling it off from what I had to do on the jump. The issues surrounding the book would be waiting for me when I landed.

When the door to the plane finally opened and I jumped into the crystal-clear blue sky over San Diego, I felt at peace. There was comfort in going through my jump procedures because I had little room in my mind to think about anything else.

What I learned almost immediately after the news report containing my name was that the skills I'd tried for more than a decade to master actually meant something in the civilian world. When I focused on them, the drama revolving around the publication of *No Easy Day* and the transition to civilian life didn't become easy, but they became manageable.

Throughout the process I kept reflecting on all the lessons that I'd learned during my career. My ability to manage stress, stay focused, and keep the problems compartmentalized kept me from losing my mind. These skills spread to the publishing team. Concepts like the "three-foot world" became part of our vocabulary.

The most gratifying part of the *No Easy Day* publication was the response from the people who read the book. Maybe the biggest surprise was that most of the readers who reached out to me wanted to talk not about the ███████████ but about the glimpses of the rest of my career and my buddies that they had found in the book.

So many people sent me inspirational accounts of challenges in their own lives and how they had overcome them, sometimes with some inspiration they had taken from *No Easy Day*. I certainly never intended that, but it makes me happy to know that the SEALs I wrote about in my first book have inspired others. It makes sense to me, because I always found inspiration in the team too. The men I served with drove me to be better, as a SEAL and as a person.

I am still trying to get my feet underneath me, but every day my path gets clearer. I fell back on what I'd learned and that is why I wanted to write this book. *No Hero* is part of my reinvention and my way to pay it forward. The book is as much for non-SEALs as it is a way to honor my brothers in the SEAL community.

These aren't only my lessons. These are lessons I've learned from mistakes I've made as well as those made by others who were willing to share their lessons with me. I've screwed up plenty of times. I'm definitely not perfect. I've tried to bring those mistakes and lessons together in one place so that maybe others can avoid them.

Getting off the speeding train was not easy. I have watched from the sidelines as my teammates, my brothers, continue to fight overseas. I read the news and follow the developments in Somalia and Iraq. My stomach hurts when I read about Fallujah being overtaken by al Qaeda because I've fought there. I sometimes wish there was something I could do.

But I have a new mission now, one that I chose. For a long time, I thought the lessons and methods we used in the military could apply only to SEALs. A lot of people I talk to think there are major differences between combat and civilian leadership, motivation, and mental toughness.

I tell them I now disagree.

Since I've transitioned out of the SEAL teams and into civilian life, I've discovered that the lessons I learned during my career apply to a much greater audience than just our community.

These lessons are fundamentals.

There is no Navy SEAL secret sauce, but if I had to make one it would be built from the basics. When you're stressed, like in combat, the simple skills are easiest to muster. Understanding the most basic principles perfectly, and working to execute them flawlessly in any circumstance, will always put you ahead of someone who lacks the fundamentals. All a SEAL does is master the basic principles and perform them as close to perfect as possible. I have found that if you remember the little things, the rest will work itself out.

Now that I've gotten out of the Navy and had time to interact with people other than SEALs, I see the chance to inspire and inform people by telling the stories that my swim buddies and I have learned in the constant drive to be the best SEALs possible. I thought telling our story was important before I wrote *No Easy Day*, and now I think it is critical.

I hope the next generation of SEALs, Delta, Rangers, and Special Forces soldiers will read this book, and *No Easy Day*, and be inspired to live a life of service like all our servicemen and women have. Maybe a few of them will carry some of my lessons learned with them onto the battlefield and be safer and more effective because of it. I know not everybody dreams of testing themselves in combat, but I think no matter what challenges you face, you can find something valuable in the stories of the men and women I served with, those still in the fight and those who've lost their lives.

I hope *No Easy Day* and *No Hero* offer something most books on war don't: the intimate side of it, the personal struggles and hardships and what we gained from them. I believe it would be irresponsible of me not to share the most intimate parts of my career in hopes that people don't have to make the same mistakes I've made. This book is one way I can continue to give back. For the rest of my life I will find other ways to pass along the lessons I learned from my teammates and hopefully inspire others like they inspired me. Leaving a career of service didn't need to end my life of service.

ABOUT THE AUTHORS

MARK OWEN is a former member of the U.S. Naval Special Warfare Development Group, commonly known as SEAL Team Six. In his many years as a Navy SEAL, he has participated in hundreds of missions around the globe, including the rescue of Captain Richard Phillips in the Indian Ocean in 2009. Owen was a team leader on Operation Neptune Spear in Abbottabad, Pakistan, on May 1, 2011, which resulted in the death of Osama bin Laden. Owen was one of the first men through the door on the third floor of the terrorist mastermind's hideout, where he witnessed Bin Laden's death. Mark Owen's account of the raid, in *No Easy Day,* remains the only accurate eyewitness account on record.

KEVIN MAURER has covered special operations forces for nine years. He has been embedded with the Special Forces in Afghanistan six times, spent a month in 2006 with special operations units in East Africa, and has embedded with U.S. forces in Iraq and Haiti. He is the author of four books, including several about special operations.